Microsoft®
WINDOWS® XP
PROFESSIONAL

ACADEMIC LEARNING SERIES

LAB MANUAL

PUBLISHED BY
Microsoft Press
A Division of Microsoft Corporation
One Microsoft Way
Redmond, Washington 98052-6399

Copyright © 2002 by Microsoft Corporation

All rights reserved. No part of the contents of this book may be reproduced or transmitted in any form or by any means without the written permission of the publisher.

Library of Congress Cataloging-in-Publication Data

MCSE Training Kit : Microsoft Windows XP Professional (Exam 70-270) / Microsoft Corporation.
    p. cm.
  Includes index.
  ISBN 0-7356-1429-6
  ISBN 0-7356-1543-8 (Academic Learning Series)
  1. Electronic data processing personnel--Certification. 2. Microsoft Windows XP. 3. Operating systems (Computers)

QA76.3 .M3283   2001
005.4'4769--dc21   2001055807

Printed and bound in the United States of America.

1 2 3 4 5 6 7 8 9   QWT   7 6 5 4 3 2

Distributed in Canada by Penguin Books Canada Limited.

A CIP catalogue record for this book is available from the British Library.

Microsoft Press books are available through booksellers and distributors worldwide. For further information about international editions, contact your local Microsoft Corporation office or contact Microsoft Press International directly at fax (425) 936-7329. Visit our Web site at www.microsoft.com/mspress. Send comments to *tkinput@microsoft.com*.

Active Directory, Microsoft, Microsoft Press, Windows, and Windows NT are either registered trademarks or trademarks of Microsoft Corporation in the United States and/or other countries. Other product and company names mentioned herein may be the trademarks of their respective owners.

The example companies, organizations, products, domain names, e-mail addresses, logos, people, places, and events depicted herein are fictitious. No association with any real company, organization, product, domain name, e-mail address, logo, person, place, or event is intended or should be inferred.

For Microsoft Press
Acquisitions Editor: Kathy Harding
Project Editor: Julie Miller

Author: Rick Wallace

For IQUAD Solutions
Project Manager: Ila Neeley
Copy Editor: Merianne Marble
Technical Editor: Rich Hillyard
Desktop Publisher: Cathy GIlmore

SubAsy Part No. X08-58517
Body Part No. X08-58518

Introduction

This Lab Manual supplements the *ALS: Microsoft Windows XP Professional* textbook. The lab exercises in this manual are designed to be performed in a classroom by a group of students under the supervision of an instructor. This is in contrast to the hands-on practice exercises in the textbook, which are designed to be performed by individual students on computers separate from the classroom. The lab exercises in this manual and the hands-on practice exercises in the textbook form an essential part of your training because it is difficult to truly understand and use the operating system and its features without first having had the opportunity to explore the menus, options, and responses.

The labs in this manual do not mirror the exercises in the textbook; the Lab Manual exercises are written for a domain environment. For Microsoft networking, a domain is a collection of computers and users that share a common database and security policy that are stored on a computer running Windows 2000 Server and configured as a domain controller. The textbook practice exercises are designed to be performed on stand-alone computers or computers running in a workgroup. A workgroup is a collection of computers grouped for sharing resources such as data and peripherals over a local area network (LAN).

The computer names, IP addresses, most shared resources, and other specific references in this Lab Manual are different from those in the textbook practice exercises. Also, because it is not possible to predict each institution's local networking requirements, there might be slight differences between the names and addresses in your classroom and those appearing in these lab exercises. Your instructor will explain any differences.

The labs are performed in a classroom that is set up as an isolated network. The instructor computer, Instructor*x* (where *x* is replaced by a number), is a Microsoft Windows 2000 domain controller. The instructor computer includes shared folders that support the lab exercises.

The Microsoft Certified Professional (MCP) exams are demanding in both the knowledge and the hands-on experience they require. Students preparing for the Microsoft certification tests can increase their competence by gaining first-hand experience in the implementation and management of Windows XP Professional. One of the best ways to become confident in the use of Windows XP Professional is to complete all the assigned labs in this manual as well as the hands-on practice exercises in the textbook.

Contents

Introduction iii

Lab 1: Installing Windows XP Professional 1

Lab 2: Joining and Logging On to a Domain, and Using the Computer Management Snap-In 15

Lab 3: Configuring TCP/IP 19

Lab 4: Configuring a DNS Client 29

Lab 5: Searching Windows 2000 Active Directory 33

Lab 6: Installing a Network Printer 35

Lab 7: Managing Printers 41

Lab 8: Managing Documents 47

Lab 9: Assigning NTFS Permissions 51

Lab 10: Managing NTFS Permissions 61

Lab 11: Managing Shared Folders 67

Lab 12: Configuring Automatic Updates and the Remote Assistance Feature 75

Lab 13: Installing Fax Services 81

Lab 14: Auditing Resources and Events 83

Lab 15: Configuring Internet Options 91

Lab 16: Using the Compressed Folders Feature 95

Lab 17: Creating Remote Shared Folders 99

Lab 18: Installing and Using the Recovery Console 107

Lab 19: Converting a Basic Disk 111

Lab 1: Installing Windows XP Professional

Objectives

After completing this lab, you will be able to

- Install Microsoft Windows XP Professional over the network or from a CD-ROM
- Log on locally to a computer running Windows XP Professional

Note Completing this lab will help reinforce your learning from Chapter 2 of the textbook.

Before You Begin

You will complete either Exercise 1 or Exercise 2. In Exercise 1, you install Windows XP Professional by using a legacy version of Microsoft Windows installed on your computer, connecting to the instructor computer, and then performing an over-the-network installation. If your instructor provides you with a *Microsoft Windows XP Professional* installation CD-ROM, complete Exercise 2 to install Windows XP Professional from a CD-ROM.

You will need to get your student ID number for your computer and the instructor number from your instructor before you begin either exercise.

Check with your instructor to find out whether or not you will be setting up Internet access on your computer.

Check with your instructor to find out whether or not you will be activating and registering your software. In the real world, you must activate and should register your copy of Windows XP Professional. However, in this classroom environment, your instructor might not have you register this copy of Windows XP Professional.

Estimated time to complete the lab: 60 minutes

Exercise 1
Installing Windows XP Professional over the Network

In this exercise, you will install Microsoft Windows XP Professional by using a legacy version of a Windows operating system and connecting to a network share on the instructor's computer to perform an over-the-network installation. The following steps are based on a computer running Microsoft Windows NT Workstation 4.

Note The steps for other legacy versions can vary slightly.

▶ **To install Windows XP Professional**

1. Start your computer and log on locally as Administrator, using a password of **password**.
2. Click the Start button, and then click Run.

   A run dialog box appears.
3. In the Open box, type **\\instructor*x*\wxppro** (where *x* is the instructor number obtained from your instructor), and then click OK.

   An Enter Network Password dialog box appears because you are not logged on to the domain and cannot access other resources on the domain.
4. In the Connect As text box, type **Student*z*** (where *z* is your student ID number), and in the Password text box, type **password**.
5. Click OK.

   A window appears, showing the folders in the wxppro share.
6. Double-click the i386 folder.

   A window appears, listing the files in the i386 folder.
7. Scroll through the listed files and locate Winnt32.

   There should be three files labeled Winnt32.
8. Point to the first file labeled Winnt32.

   It should be the stub loader for the Winnt32 Setup Program.
9. Double-click the stub loader for the Winnt32 Setup Program.

   Setup displays the Welcome To Windows Setup screen.
10. In the Installation Type box, select New Installation (Advanced), and then click Next.

    Setup displays the License Agreement screen.

Lab 1: Installing Windows XP Professional

11. Read the license agreement, select I Accept This Agreement, and then click Next.

    Setup displays the Your Product Key screen. Your instructor will give you the product key you should use.

12. Type your 25-character product key, and then click Next.

    Setup displays the Setup Options screen, which allows you to configure the following three options:

    - Advanced, which allows you to control where the installation files are obtained, where the installation files are copied to, whether to copy all installation files from the *Microsoft Windows XP Professional* CD-ROM to the hard disk, and whether you want to specify the drive letter and partition during Setup

    - Accessibility, which gives you the option of using the Microsoft Magnifier during setup to display an enlarged portion of the screen in a separate window (for users with limited vision) and the option of using the Microsoft Narrator to read the contents of the screen (for users who are blind)

    - Select The Primary Language And Region You Want To Use, which allows you to specify the primary language and region to use

13. After you have configured any required Setup options, click Next.

    Setup displays the Get Updated Setup Files dialog box.

Note If your computer has Internet access, you might want to ensure that the Yes, Download The Updated Setup Files (Recommended) check box is selected, and then click Next.

---

14. Select No, Skip This Step And Continue Installing Windows, and then click Next.

    If your partition is not currently formatted with the Windows XP Professional NT file system (NTFS), the Setup Wizard displays the Upgrade To The Windows NTFS File System screen.

15. If you get the Upgrade To The Windows NTFS File System screen, ensure that Yes, Upgrade My Drive is selected, and then click Next.

    Setup displays the Welcome To Setup screen.

Note You can also use this method to access the Recovery Console to repair an existing Windows XP Professional installation by pressing R. You can quit the installation by pressing F3.

▶ **To run the Setup Wizard**

1. On the Welcome To Setup screen, press ENTER to install Windows XP Professional.

   The Setup program prompts you to select an area of free space or an existing partition to install Windows XP Professional in.

   Note You can also delete partitions at this time. If you have a C partition, you might not be able to delete it because Setup has already loaded some files onto it. The partition you choose must be at least 2000 MB in size. If you cannot use the C partition (drive C) to install Windows XP Professional, you must replace the C partition (drive C) in all the following labs in this course with the appropriate partition (or drive letter), the one you install Windows XP Professional on.

2. Select the C partition.

   Setup displays the following message: You chose to install Windows XP on a partition that contains another operating system. Installing Windows XP Professional on this partition might cause the other operating system to function improperly.

3. Press C to have Setup continue and use this partition.

   Caution Depending on the operating system currently installed on the C partition, Setup might display the following message: A \WINDOWS folder already exists that may contain a Windows installation. If you continue the existing Windows installation will be overwritten. If you want to keep both operating systems, press Esc and specify a different folder to use.

4. If you get a warning that a \WINDOWS folder already exists, press L to use the folder and delete the installation in it.

   If your partition was not formatted with NTFS and you chose to have the partition formatted with NTFS, Setup now formats it as NTFS and then copies files. Otherwise, Setup examines the partition and then copies files.

   Setup reboots the computer and continues to copy files in GUI mode. This might take several minutes. A status page gives time-to-completion estimates.

   The Setup Wizard displays the Regional And Language Options page so that you can customize Windows XP Professional for different regions and languages.

5. Select the appropriate standards and formats, text input language, and keyboard layout (or ensure that they are correct for your language and location), and then click Next.

The Setup Wizard displays the Personalize Your Software page, prompting you for your name and organization name. Setup uses your organization name to generate the default computer name. Many applications that you install later will use this information for product registration and document identification.

6. In the Name box, type your name. In the Organization box, type the name of your organization or school, and then click Next.

   The Setup Wizard displays the Computer Name And Administrator Password page.

7. In the Computer Name box, type **Computerz** (where z is your student ID number).

Note Windows XP Professional displays the name in all uppercase letters no matter how you type it.

8. In the Administrator Password box and in the Confirm Password box, type **password** and then click Next.

Important For the labs in this course, you will use **password** for the Administrator account. In the real world, you should always use a complex password for the Administrator account (one that others cannot easily guess). Microsoft recommends mixing uppercase and lowercase letters, numbers, and symbols (for example, Lp6*g9F2).

Depending on your computer configuration, the Setup Wizard might display the Modem Dialing Information page.

Note If the Setup Wizard does not display the Modem Dialing Information page, it is probably because a modem is not installed on your computer. In that case, skip to step 13.

9. Ensure that the correct country or region is selected.
10. Type the correct area code or city code.
11. If you dial a number to get an outside line, type that number.
12. Ensure that the correct dialing type (Tone or Pulse) is selected, and then click Next.

    The Setup Wizard displays the Date And Time Settings page.

13. If necessary, select the time zone for your location from the time zone drop-down list, and adjust the date and time.
14. Ensure that the Automatically Adjust For Daylight Saving Changes check box is selected if you want Windows XP Professional to automatically adjust the time on your computer for daylight saving time, and then click Next.

> **Note** If you have configured your computer for dual booting with another operating system that can also adjust your clock for daylight saving time, enable this feature for the operating system that you use most frequently so that the time adjustment will occur only once.

The Setup Wizard continues copying files and then displays the Networking Settings page.

▶ **To install Windows Networking**

1. Ensure that Typical Settings is selected, and then click Next.

   The Setup Wizard displays the Workgroup Or Computer Domain page.

> **Note** Normally, when you install Windows XP Professional on a computer, you would join a domain at this point of the installation. For purposes of this class, you will not join a domain until later in the course.

2. Ensure that No, This Computer Is Not On A Network, Or Is On A Network Without A Domain is selected and that the workgroup name is WORKGROUP, and then click Next.

   The Setup Wizard configures the networking components and then copies files. This process takes several minutes.

▶ **To complete the installation**

After the Setup Wizard installs the networking components, it automatically starts the final step in the installation process. The Setup Wizard installs Start menu items, registers components, saves settings, and removes temporary files. This process takes several minutes.

The computer restarts, and the Setup Wizard displays the Welcome To Microsoft Windows page.

1. Click Next to continue.

   The Setup Wizard displays the How Will This Computer Connect To The Internet page.

> **Note** Your instructor will tell you whether or not to connect to the Internet.

2. If you do not want to connect to the Internet at this time, click Skip. If you do want to set up an Internet connection, select the appropriate connection method, and then click Next. Then follow the instructions on the screen and from your instructor to set up your Internet connection.

   The Setup Wizard displays the Ready To Activate Windows page.

Important You must activate Windows XP Professional either during installation or within 30 days of installation. If you are not going to activate Windows XP Professional now, select No, Remind Me Every Few Days, and then skip to step 6. If you are going to activate, go to step 3.

3. Select Yes, Activate Windows Over The Internet Now, and then click Next.

   The Setup Wizard displays the Ready To Register With Microsoft page.

Important Did you verify with your instructor whether or not you are to register this copy of Windows XP Professional? In the real world, you should register your copy of Windows XP Professional, but in this classroom environment, your instructor might not have you register this copy of Windows XP Professional.

4. If your instructor told you to register this copy of Windows XP Professional, select Yes, I'd Like To Register With Microsoft Now, and then click Next.

   The Setup Wizard displays the Collecting Registration Information page.

5. Fill in the appropriate text boxes, and then click Next.

   The Setup Wizard displays the Ready To Send Information page.

6. Click Next.

   If you set up your Internet connection (in step 2), the Setup Wizard displays the Do You Want To Set Up Internet Access Now page, which allows you to set up a connection to an Internet service provider (ISP).

Note A connection to an ISP is not required for this course. Your instructor will tell you whether or not to set up access to an ISP. If you do not want to set up Internet access, go to step 7. If you do want to set up access to an ISP at this time, check Yes, Help Me Connect To The Internet, and then click Next and follow the instructions on the screen and from your instructor.

7. If you do not want to set up access to an ISP, select No, Not At This Time, and then click Next.

   The Setup Wizard displays the Who Will Use This Computer page. Your name should already be entered.

8. Type **Fred** for the second user, and then click Next.

   The Setup Wizard displays the Thank You page.

9. Read the page, and then click Finish.

10. To log on, click Fred (or the account name created for you during installation).

    You have now completed your installation of Windows XP Professional and logged on to the local computer as an administrator.

Exercise 2
Installing Windows XP Professional from a CD-ROM

In this exercise, you will install Microsoft Windows XP Professional from a CD-ROM on a computer that contains no partitions or operating systems.

▶ **To run the Setup program**

1. Insert the *Microsoft Windows XP Professional* CD-ROM into the CD-ROM drive and turn the computer on.

Important Your computer must be able to boot from a CD-ROM to perform this exercise. Some computers require you to press a key to boot from the CD-ROM drive. If you are prompted to press any key, press the SPACEBAR. If you are prompted to press a key to boot from the CD-ROM, you only have a few seconds to press a key. If you do not press a key fast enough, the computer will not boot from the CD-ROM. You must reboot your computer and be ready to press the SPACEBAR quickly.

Setup displays the Windows Setup screen while it is loading files, and then displays the Windows XP Professional Setup screen.

Note You can also use the Windows XP Professional Setup program to repair or recover a damaged Windows XP Professional installation.

2. Read the Welcome To Setup screen, and then press ENTER to set up Windows XP Professional now.

   Setup displays the Windows XP Licensing Agreement screen.

3. Read the licensing agreement, and then press F8 to agree with the licensing terms.

   Setup displays another screen, which prompts you to create a partition to install Windows XP Professional into.

Important You must create a space of at least 2000 MB in size.

4. Select an area of unpartitioned space, at least 2000 MB in size, and press C.

   Setup prompts you to enter a size for the partition.

Note If you want to use only a portion of the available space, enter the amount of space you want to use, and then press ENTER.

5. Type a size for the partition that leaves about 50 MB of free space, and then press ENTER.

For example, if your unpartitioned space is 2000 MB in size, then the size you type for the partition is 1950 MB. If your unpartitioned space is 2950 MB in size, then the size you type for the partition is 2900 MB.

Note If your partitions are already created, you can also delete partitions at this time. If you have a C partition, you might not be able to delete it because Setup has already loaded some files on it.

Setup displays the list of existing partitions for you to select a partition for the installation.

6. Press ENTER to install Windows XP Professional on the partition you created.

   Because you are installing into a newly created, unformatted partition, Windows XP Professional Setup prompts you to format the partition.

Caution If you are planning on dual booting your computer with an operating system that does not support the NT file system (NTFS), drive C cannot be formatted with NTFS. You might want to install Windows XP Professional on a different drive and format that drive with NTFS.

7. When prompted, select Format The Partition Using The NTFS File System.

Note Since this is a new (or "raw") partition, you cannot do a quick format, so you cannot select Format The Partition Using The NTFS File System (Quick).

The formatting will take several minutes; the larger the partition size, the longer the formatting will take.

Note If you format the partition with the file allocation table (FAT) file system, Windows XP Professional provides the Convert command, which you can use to convert a partition to NTFS after installation is complete without reformatting the partitions and losing all the information contained on the partition.

After Setup formats the partition, Setup examines the hard drive, and then copies files to the Windows installation folders.

8. When Setup prompts you to restart the computer, remove the CD-ROM from the CD-ROM drive, and then press ENTER.

   Pressing ENTER saves you a few seconds of time. If you don't press ENTER, Setup will automatically reboot the computer.

Important If you do not remove the *Microsoft Windows XP Professional* CD-ROM from the CD-ROM drive and your computer attempts to reboot from the CD-ROM, remove the CD-ROM and then restart the computer.

The computer restarts. If you removed the CD-ROM, a message box appears, prompting you to insert the *Microsoft Windows XP Professional* CD-ROM into your CD-ROM drive.

▶ **To run the Setup Wizard**

1. If you removed the CD-ROM, insert the *Microsoft Windows XP Professional* CD-ROM into your CD-ROM drive, and then click OK.

   Windows XP Professional installs the files and devices. This might take several minutes. A status screen gives time-to-completion estimates.

   Note It is normal for your screen to flicker during this part of the installation.

   The Setup Wizard displays the Regional And Language Options page so that you can customize Windows XP Professional for different regions and languages.

2. Select the appropriate standards and formats, text input language, and keyboard layout (or ensure that they are correct for your language and location), and then click Next.

   The Setup Wizard displays the Personalize Your Software page, prompting you for your name and organization name. Setup uses your organization name to generate the default computer name. Many applications that you install later will use this information for product registration and document identification.

3. In the Name box, type your name. In the Organization box, type the name of your organization or school, and then click Next.

   The Setup Wizard displays the Your Product Key page.

4. Type your 25-character product key, located on the back of your *Microsoft Windows XP Professional* CD-ROM case, and then click Next.

   The Setup Wizard displays the Computer Name And Administrator Password page.

5. In the Computer Name box, type **Computer**z (where z is your student ID number).

   Note Windows XP Professional displays the name in all uppercase letters no matter how you type it.

6. In the Administrator Password box and in the Confirm Password box, type **password** and then click Next.

Important For the labs in this course, you will use **password** for the Administrator account. In the real world, you should always use a complex password for the Administrator account (one that others cannot easily guess). Microsoft recommends mixing uppercase and lowercase letters, numbers, and symbols (for example, Lp6*g9F2).

Depending on your computer configuration, the Setup Wizard might display the Modem Dialing Information page.

Note If the Setup Wizard does not display the Modem Dialing Information page, it is probably because a modem is not installed on your computer. In that case, skip to step 11.

7. Ensure that the correct country or region is selected.
8. Type the correct area code or city code.
9. If you dial a number to get an outside line, type the number.
10. Ensure that the correct dialing type (Tone or Pulse) is selected, and then click Next.

    The Setup Wizard displays the Date And Time Settings page.
11. If necessary, select the time zone for your location from the Time Zone drop-down list, and adjust the date and time.
12. Ensure that the Automatically Adjust For Daylight Saving Changes check box is selected if you want Windows XP Professional to automatically adjust the time on your computer for daylight saving time, and then click Next.

Note If you have configured your computer for dual booting with another operating system that can also adjust your clock for daylight saving time, enable this feature for the operating system that you use most frequently so that the time adjustment will occur only once.

The Setup Wizard continues copying files and then displays the Networking Settings page.

▶ **To install Windows Networking**

1. Ensure that Typical Settings is selected, and then click Next.

   The Setup Wizard displays the Workgroup Or Computer Domain page.

Note Normally, when you install Windows XP Professional, you would join a domain at this point of the installation. For purposes of this class, you will not join a domain until later in the course.

2. Ensure that No, This Computer Is Not On A Network, Or Is On A Network Without A Domain is selected and that the workgroup name is WORKGROUP, and then click Next.

   The Setup Wizard configures the networking components and then copies files. This process takes several minutes.

▶ **To complete the installation**

After the Setup Wizard installs the networking components, it automatically starts the final step in the installation process. The Setup Wizard installs Start menu items, registers components, saves settings, and removes temporary files. This process takes several minutes.

The computer restarts, and the Setup Wizard displays the Welcome To Microsoft Windows page.

Important If your computer attempts to reboot from the *Microsoft Windows XP Professional* CD-ROM, remove the CD-ROM and then restart the computer.

1. Click Next to continue.

   The Setup Wizard displays the How Will This Computer Connect To The Internet page.

Note Your instructor will tell you whether or not to connect to the Internet.

2. If you do not want to connect to the Internet at this time, click Skip. If you do want to set up an Internet connection, select the appropriate connection method, and then click Next. Then follow the instructions on the screen and from your instructor for setting up your Internet connection.

   The Setup Wizard displays the Ready To Activate Windows page.

Important You must activate Windows XP Professional either during installation or within 30 days of installation. If you are not going to activate Windows XP Professional now, select No, Remind Me Every Few Days, and then skip to step 6. If you are going to activate, go to step 3.

3. Select Yes, Activate Windows Over The Internet Now, and then click Next.

   The Setup Wizard displays the Ready To Register With Microsoft page.

Important Did you verify with your instructor whether or not you are to register this copy of Windows XP Professional? In the real world, you should register your copy of Windows XP Professional, but in this classroom environment, your instructor might not have you register this copy of Windows XP Professional.

4. If your instructor told you to register this copy of Windows XP Professional, select Yes, I'd Like To Register With Microsoft Now, and then click Next.

   The Setup Wizard displays the Collecting Registration Information page.

5. Fill in the appropriate text boxes, and then click Next.

   The Setup Wizard displays the Ready To Send Information page.

6. Click Next.

   If you set up your Internet connection (in step 2), the Setup Wizard displays the Do You Want To Set Up Internet Access Now page, which allows you to set up a connection to an Internet service provider (ISP).

Note A connection to an ISP is not required for this course. Your instructor will tell you whether or not to set up access to an ISP. If you do not want to set up Internet access, go to step 7. If you do want to set up access to an ISP at this time, select Yes, Help Me Connect To The Internet, and then click Next and follow the instructions on the screen and from your instructor.

7. If you do not want to set up access to an ISP, select No, Not At This Time, and then click Next.

   The Setup Wizard displays the Who Will Use This Computer page. Your name should already be entered.

8. Type **Fred** for the second user, and then click Next.

   The Setup Wizard displays the Thank You page.

9. Read the page, and then click Finish.

10. To log on, click Fred (or the account name created for you during installation).

    You have now completed your installation of Windows XP Professional and logged on to the local computer as an administrator.

Lab 2: Joining and Logging On to a Domain, and Using the Computer Management Snap-In

Objectives

After completing this lab, you will be able to

- Join your computer to a domain
- Log on to a domain
- Create a local user account on your computer, using the Computer Management snap-in

Note Completing this lab will help reinforce your learning from Chapter 3 of the textbook.

Before You Begin

In Exercise 1, you join your computer to the Corpy domain. In Exercise 2, you log on to the Corpy domain. In Exercise 3, you use the Computer Management snap-in to view the existing local user accounts and to create a new local user account.

Note Microsoft does not recommend using local user accounts in a domain environment. This lab is included so you can learn how to add your computer to a domain. The lab shows you how to log on to a domain and to a local computer that is a member of that domain. While logged on to the local computer, you will create a local user account, using the Computer Management snap-in. (The exercises in the textbook that you will do as homework will familiarize you with using the User Accounts tool in the workgroup environment to create local user accounts).

Ensure that you know your student ID number for your computer and the domain number. You can get this information from your instructor.

Estimated time to complete the lab: 15 minutes

Exercise 1
Joining a Domain

In this exercise, you will join your computer to the Corpy domain.

▶ **To join a domain**

1. Log on to your computer as Fred by clicking on the icon for Fred.
2. Click Start, right-click My Computer, and then click Properties.

    The System Properties dialog box appears, with the General tab selected.

3. Click the Computer Name tab.

    Notice that your computer name is Computerz (where z is your student ID number) and that it is currently a member of the workgroup named WORKGROUP.

4. Click Change.

    The Computer Name Changes dialog box appears.

5. Under Member Of, click Domain and then type **Corpy** in the text box (where y is the domain number that your instructor told you to use).

6. Click OK.

    Another Computer Name Changes dialog box appears, prompting you to enter the name and password of an account with permission to join the domain.

    Your instructor has already set up a domain user account for you, with the user name Studentz (where z is your student ID number) and a password of password (which you should never change for the class).

7. In the User Name text box, type **Studentz** (where z is your student ID number), and in the Password text box, type **password**.

    A Computer Name Changes message box appears, welcoming you to the Corpy domain.

8. Click OK to close the message box.

    Another Computer Name Changes message box appears, telling you that you must restart your computer.

9. Click OK to close the message box.
10. Click OK to close the System Properties dialog box.

    A System Settings Change message box appears, asking you if you want to restart your computer now.

11. Click Yes to restart your computer.

    Your computer is now a member of the corpy.corp.com domain.

Exercise 2
Logging On to the Corp*y* Domain

In this exercise, you will log on to the Corp*y* domain (where *y* is the domain number).

Note When you switch from a workgroup environment to a domain environment, the way you log on to the computer changes. The Welcome To Windows message box prompts you to press CTRL+ALT+DELETE.

▶ **To log on to the domain**

1. At the Welcome to Windows message box, press CTRL+ALT+DELETE.

   The Log On To Windows dialog box appears.

2. In the Log On To Windows dialog box, click Options.

   The Log On To Windows dialog box displays additional options, including a Log On To text box.

3. In the User Name text box, type **Student*z*** (where *z* is your student ID number), and in the Password box, type **password**.

   Notice the Log On Using Dial-Up Connection check box. This check box lets a user connect to a domain server by using dial-up networking. There is also a Shut Down button that you can click to shut down the computer.

4. Click the down arrow at the end of the Log On To drop-down list.

   What are the available selections in the Log On To list?

   _____

   _____

5. In the Log On To list, select Corp*y*, and then click OK.

   You are now logged on to the Corp*y* domain.

6. To log off the domain, click Start, click Log Off, and in the Log Off Windows dialog box, click Log Off.

Exercise 3
Using the Computer Management Snap-In to Create a Local User Account

In this exercise, even though your computer is in a domain environment, you log on to the local computer. You will log on to your local computer and use the Computer Management snap-in to create a local user account on your computer.

▶ **To create a local user account on your computer**

1. At the Welcome to Windows message box, press CTRL+ALT+DELETE.

    The Log On To Windows dialog box appears.

2. In the User Name text box, type **Fred**.
3. In the Log On To text box, select Computer$z$ (where z is your student ID number).

    For this exercise, you want to log on to the local computer, not the domain.

4. Click Start, right-click My Computer, and click Manage.

    The Computer Management snap-in appears.

5. If necessary, expand System Tools, and then expand Local Users And Tools.
6. Right-click Users, and then click New User.
7. In the User Name text box, type **User40** and in the Full Name text box, type **User Forty**.
8. In the Password text box and the Confirm Password text box, type **password**.
9. Clear the User Must Change Password At Next Logon check box.
10. Select the Password Never Expires check box.
11. Click Create to create the user account.
12. Click Close to close the New User dialog box.

    In the details pane, notice that User40 has been created as a local user account. You might need to expand the Users folder to see a list of the users.

Note Microsoft does not recommend using local user accounts in a domain environment. The local user accounts are stored on the local security database on a computer, while the domain user accounts are stored in the Active Directory service on the domain controllers for the domain. Using local user accounts undermines the centralized administration that domains provide. You will learn more about Active Directory in Chapter 5 of the textbook, "Using the DNS Service and Active Directory Service."

13. On the File menu, click Exit.
14. Log off the computer.

Lab 3: Configuring TCP/IP

Objectives

After completing this lab, you will be able to

- Verify a computer's Transmission Control Protocol/Internet Protocol (TCP/IP) configuration
- Configure TCP/IP to use a static Internet Protocol (IP) address, using Automatic IP Addressing
- Configure TCP/IP to obtain an IP address automatically, using Dynamic Host Configuration Protocol (DHCP)
- Verify that an IP address was assigned by Automatic Private IP Addressing and test connectivity
- Determine what happens when there is no server running the DHCP Service to provide an IP address

Note Completing this lab will help reinforce your learning from Chapter 4 of the textbook.

Before You Begin

In this lab, you will be working with a lab partner in some of the exercises. Get your lab partner assignment from your instructor.

Tip As you complete the exercises in this lab, you will use the command prompt and Network Connections windows frequently. For the sake of efficiency, open the windows just one time, and then minimize and restore them as necessary.

Estimated time to complete the lab: 50 minutes

Exercise 1
Verifying a Computer's TCP/IP Configuration

In this exercise, you will use two TCP/IP tools, Ipconfig and Ping, to verify your computer's configuration.

▶ **To verify a computer's configuration**

1. Log on locally to your computer as Fred, who is a member of the Administrators group.
2. Click Start, and then click Run.
3. In the Run dialog box, type **cmd** and then click OK to open a command prompt.
4. At the command prompt, type **ipconfig /all | more** and then press ENTER.

   The Microsoft Windows XP Professional IP Configuration tool displays the TCP/IP configuration of the physical and logical adapters configured on your computer.
5. Press SPACEBAR as necessary to display the Local Area Connection heading. Use the information displayed in this section to complete as much of the following table as possible. Press SPACEBAR to display additional information as necessary and to return to the command prompt.

Local area connection setting	Value
Host name	
Primary DNS suffix	
Connection-specific DNS suffix description	
Physical address	
DHCP enabled	
Autoconfiguration enabled	
Autoconfiguration IP address	
Subnet mask	
Default gateway	

6. To verify that the IP address is working and configured for your adapter, type **ping 127.0.0.1** and then press ENTER.

Note You can also ping the IP address of your computer's network adapter to verify that the IP address is working and configured for your adapter.

A response similar to the following indicates a successful ping:

```
Pinging 127.0.0.1 with 32 bytes of data:
Reply from 127.0.0.1: bytes=32 time<10ms TTL=128
Reply from 127.0.0.1: bytes=32 time<10ms TTL=128
Reply from 127.0.0.1: bytes=32 time<10ms TTL=128
Reply from 127.0.0.1: bytes=32 time<10ms TTL=128
Ping statistics for 127.0.0.1:
Packets: Sent = 4, Received = 4, Lost = 0 <0% loss>,
Approximate round trip times in milliseconds:
Minimum = 0ms, Maximum = 0ms, Average = 0ms
```

7. Minimize the command prompt window.

Exercise 2
Configuring TCP/IP to Use a Static IP Address

In this exercise, you will configure TCP/IP to use a static IP address, and then you will verify your computer's new configuration.

▶ **To configure TCP/IP to use a static IP address**

1. Click Start, and then click Control Panel.
2. In the Control Panel window, click Network And Internet Connections.
3. In the Network And Internet Connections window, click Network Connections, and then click Local Area Connection.
4. Under Network Tasks, click Change Settings Of This Connection.

   The Local Area Connection Properties dialog box appears, displaying the network adapter in use and the network components used in this connection.
5. In the General tab, click Internet Protocol (TCP/IP), and then verify that the check box to the left of the entry is selected.
6. Click Properties.

   The Internet Protocol (TCP/IP) Properties dialog box appears.
7. Click Use The Following IP Address.

Important In the next step, enter the IP address, subnet mask, and default gateway values you recorded in the table in Exercise 1.

8. In the IP Address text box, type the IP address you recorded in the table in Exercise 1.
9. In the Subnet Mask text box, type the subnet mask that you recorded in the table in Exercise 1.

Important Be careful when entering IP configuration settings manually, especially numeric addresses. The most frequent cause of TCP/IP connection problems is incorrectly entered IP address information.

10. In the Default Gateway text box, type the default gateway you recorded in the table in Exercise 1.
11. Click OK to return to the Local Area Connection Properties dialog box.
12. Click OK to close the Local Area Connection Properties dialog box and return to the Network Connections window.
13. Minimize the Network Connections window.

▶ **To test the static TCP/IP configuration**

1. Restore the command prompt window.

2. At the command prompt, type **ipconfig /all | more** and then press ENTER.

   The Windows XP Professional IP Configuration tool displays the physical and logical adapters configured on your computer.

3. Press SPACEBAR as needed to scroll through the configuration information and locate the local area connection information.

4. Record the current TCP/IP configuration settings for your local area connection in the following table.

Setting	Value
IP address	
Subnet mask	
Default gateway	

5. Press SPACEBAR as necessary to scroll through the configuration information and return to the command prompt.

6. To verify that the IP address is working and configured for your adapter, type **ping 127.0.0.1** and then press ENTER.

   If the address is working and configured, you receive the following result:

   ```
   Reply from 127.0.0.1: bytes=32 time<1ms TTL=128
   Reply from 127.0.0.1: bytes=32 time<1ms TTL=128
   Reply from 127.0.0.1: bytes=32 time<1ms TTL=128
   Reply from 127.0.0.1: bytes=32 time<1ms TTL=128
   Ping statistics for 127.0.0.1:
   Packets: Sent = 4, Received = 4, Lost = 0 <0% loss>,
   Approximate round trip times in milliseconds:
   Minimum = 0ms, Maximum = 0ms, Average = 0ms
   ```

7. Type **ping** *ip_address* (where *ip_address* is the IP address of your lab partner's computer), and then press ENTER.

   If your lab partner's computer TCP/IP address is working and configured, you receive the following result:

   ```
   Reply from ip_address: bytes=32 time<1ms TTL=128
   Reply from ip_address: bytes=32 time<1ms TTL=128
   Reply from ip_address: bytes=32 time<1ms TTL=128
   Reply from ip_address: bytes=32 time<1ms TTL=128
   Ping statistics for ip_address:
   Packets: Sent = 4, Received = 4, Lost = 0 <0% loss>,
   Approximate round trip times in milliseconds:
   Minimum = 0ms, Maximum = 0ms, Average = 0ms
   ```

8. Minimize the command prompt window.

Exercise 3
Configuring TCP/IP to Obtain an IP Address Automatically

In this exercise, you will configure TCP/IP to obtain an IP address automatically. Then you will test the configuration to verify that the DHCP Service has provided the appropriate IP addressing information.

▶ **To configure TCP/IP to obtain an IP address automatically**

1. Restore the Network Connections window, right-click Local Area Connection, and then click Properties.

    The Local Area Connection Properties dialog box appears.

2. In the General tab, click Internet Protocol (TCP/IP), and verify that the check box to the left of the entry is selected.

3. Click Properties.

    The Internet Protocol (TCP/IP) Properties dialog box appears.

4. Click Obtain An IP Address Automatically.
5. Click Obtain DNS Server Address Automatically.
6. Click OK to close the Internet Protocol (TCP/IP) Properties dialog box.
7. Click OK to close the Local Area Connection Properties dialog box.
8. Minimize the Network Connections window.

▶ **To test the TCP/IP configuration**

Note If there is not a server running the DHCP Service to provide an IP address, skip this procedure and continue with Exercise 4.

1. Restore the command prompt window, type **ipconfig /release** and then press ENTER.
2. At the command prompt, type **ipconfig /renew** and then press ENTER.
3. At the command prompt, type **ipconfig | more** and then press ENTER.
4. Pressing SPACEBAR as necessary, record the current TCP/IP configuration settings for your local area connection in the following table.

Setting	Value
IP address	
Subnet mask	
Default gateway	

5. To test that TCP/IP is working and bound to your adapter, type **ping 127.0.0.1** and then press ENTER.

   The internal loopback test displays four replies if TCP/IP is bound to the adapter.

Exercise 4
Obtaining an IP Address by Using Automatic Private IP Addressing

Before you begin this exercise, you will need to make sure that your instructor has disabled the DHCP Service so that no DHCP servers are available to provide an IP address for your computer. Without a DHCP server available to provide an IP address, the Windows XP Professional Automatic Private IP Addressing feature provides unique IP addresses for your computer. If the DHCP Service cannot be disabled, simply disconnect your network adapter cable.

▶ **To obtain an IP address by using Automatic Private IP Addressing**

1. At the command prompt, type **ipconfig /release** and then press ENTER.
2. At the command prompt, type **ipconfig /renew** and then press ENTER.

    There is a pause while Windows XP Professional attempts to locate a DHCP server on the network.

    What does the message that appears indicate?

    _____

    _____

3. Click OK to close the dialog box.

▶ **To test the TCP/IP configuration**

1. At the command prompt, type **ipconfig | more** and then press ENTER.
2. Press SPACEBAR as necessary, and record the current TCP/IP settings for your local area connection in the following table.

Setting	Value
IP address	_____
Subnet mask	_____
Default gateway	_____

Is this the same IP address assigned to your computer in Exercise 3? Why or why not?

_____

_____

_____

3. Press SPACEBAR as necessary to finish scrolling through the configuration information.
4. To verify that TCP/IP is working and bound to your adapter, type **ping 127.0.0.1** and then press ENTER.

   The internal loopback test displays four replies if TCP/IP is bound to the adapter.
5. Type **ping *ip_address*** (where *ip_address* is the IP address of your lab partner's computer) and then press ENTER.

   Were you successful in pinging your partner's computer? Why or why not?

   _____

   _____

   _____

Exercise 5
Obtaining an IP Address by Using DHCP

Before you begin this exercise, you will need to make sure that your instructor has enabled the DHCP Service running on the computer that is acting as a DHCP server. In this exercise, your computer obtains IP addressing information from the DHCP server.

▶ **To obtain an IP address by using DHCP**

1. At the command prompt, type **ipconfig /release** and then press ENTER.
2. At the command prompt, type **ipconfig /renew** and then press ENTER.

    After a short wait, a message box indicates that a new IP address was assigned.
3. Click OK to close the message box.
4. At the command prompt, type **ipconfig /all | more** and then press ENTER.
5. Verify that the DHCP server has assigned an IP address to your computer.
6. Close the command prompt window.

Lab 4: Configuring a DNS Client

Objectives

After completing this lab, you will be able to

- Configure a computer running Microsoft Windows XP Professional as a Domain Name System (DNS) client
- Configure DNS server addresses

Note Completing this lab will help reinforce your learning from Chapter 5 of the textbook.

Before You Begin

In this lab, you'll configure a DNS client. You'll also configure for additional DNS servers that the client could use and review the advanced configuration options that are available.

Ask your instructor to provide you with the Internet Protocol (IP) address of one or more DNS servers if they are available.

To complete this lab, you need Transmission Control Protocol/Internet Protocol (TCP/IP) installed on the computer

Estimated time to complete the lab: 15 minutes

Exercise 1
Configuring a DNS Client

In this exercise, you'll configure your Windows XP Professional computer as a DNS client by specifying the IP address of one or more DNS servers that are available on your network. You will also look at other options that can be configured for a DNS client.

▶ **To configure a DNS client**

1. Log on to your local computer as Fred.
2. Click Start, and then click Control Panel.
3. In the Control Panel window, click Network And Internet Connections.
4. In the Network And Internet Connections window, click Network Connections.
5. In the Network Connections window, right-click Local Area Connection, and then click Properties.
6. Click Internet Protocol (TCP/IP).

   There should still be a check mark in the check box to the left of Internet Protocol (TCP/IP).

7. Click Properties.

   The Internet Protocol (TCP/IP) Properties dialog box appears.

   If the Obtain An IP Address Automatically option is selected, as it is by default, notice that the Preferred DNS Server text box and the Alternate DNS Server check box are unavailable (grayed out).

8. Click Use The Following DNS Server Addresses.

   The Preferred DNS Server text box and the Alternate DNS Server text box are now available.

   Note Your instructor will provide you with the IP address of one or more DNS servers if they are available.

9. In the Preferred DNS Server text box, type the IP address of a DNS server.
10. If a second DNS server is available, in the Alternate DNS Server text box, type the IP address of the second DNS server.
11. Click Advanced.

    The Advanced TCP/IP Settings dialog box appears.

Note You can add addresses for additional default gateways in the Advanced TCP/IP Settings dialog box.

12. In the Advanced TCP/IP Settings dialog box, click DNS.

    Notice that the preferred and alternate DNS server IP addresses are listed and that you can add addresses for additional DNS servers.

13. Click Add.

    Notice that you can add additional DNS servers to the list of DNS servers for this computer to use.

14. Click Cancel.

    Notice that the Register This Connection's Addresses In DNS check box is selected.

15. Click Help (the question mark icon in the upper right-hand corner of the dialog box), and then click Register This Connection's Addresses In DNS.

    What is the function of this check box?

    _____

    _____

16. Click Cancel to close the Advanced TCP/IP Settings dialog box.
17. Click Cancel to close the Internet Protocol (TCP/IP) dialog box.
18. Click Cancel to close the Local Area Connections dialog box.
19. Close the Network Connections window.

Lab 5: Searching Windows 2000 Active Directory

Objectives

After completing this lab, you will be able to

- Search the Active Directory service for a specific computer
- Search Active Directory for a specific user

Note Completing this lab will help reinforce your learning from Chapter 5 of the textbook.

Before You Begin

In this lab, your computer should be a member of the Corpy domain. You'll log on to the domain and search Active Directory.

You will need to get your student ID number, your lab partner's student ID number, the domain number, and the instructor number from your instructor before you begin work on the lab.

Estimated time to complete the lab: 15 minutes

Exercise 1
Searching Active Directory

In this exercise, you'll log on to the Corp*y* domain.

▶ **To search Active Directory**

1. Log on to the Corp*y* domain as **Student*z*** with a password of **password** (where *y* is the domain number your instructor told you to use, and *z* is your student ID number).
2. Click Start, and then click Control Panel.
3. Click Network And Internet Connections, and then click My Network Places.
4. Under Network Tasks, click Search Active Directory.

   The Find Users, Contacts, And Groups dialog box appears.
5. Click the down arrow at the end of the Find text box, and then click Computers.
6. In the Computer Name text box, type **Instructor*x*** (where *x* is the number of the instructor's computer).

   Note You can use an asterisk (*) as a wildcard (for one or more characters). If you enter a partial name in any of these fields (even without a trailing asterisk), all names beginning with those letters will be displayed. If you do not enter any text, all the items in the given category are displayed. If you have time, experiment with using wildcards to locate objects in Active Directory.

7. Click Find Now.
8. Double-click Instructor*x*.

   You have just searched Active Directory for and located a computer.
9. Close the Instructor*x* Properties window.
10. In the Computer Name text box, type **Computer*p*** (where *p* is your lab partner's student ID number).
11. Click Find Now.
12. Click the down arrow at the end of the Find text box, and then click Users, Contacts, And Groups.
13. In the Name text box, type **Student*p*** (where *p* is your lab partner's student ID number).
14. Click Find Now.

    You have just searched Active Directory for and located a user.
15. Close the Find Users, Contacts, And Groups dialog box.
16. Close all open windows.

Lab 6: Installing a Network Printer

Objectives

After completing this lab, you will be able to

- Use the Add Printer Wizard to install and share a local printer
- Take a printer offline and then print a document, which loads the document into the print queue

Note Completing this lab will help reinforce your learning from Chapter 6 of the textbook.

Before You Begin

In this lab, you use the Add Printer Wizard to install and share a local printer. Sharing the printer makes it available to other users on the network.

You do not have to have a printer to complete this lab.

Estimated time to complete the lab: 15 minutes

Exercise 1
Adding and Sharing a Local Printer

In this exercise, you will use the Add Printer Wizard to install and share a local printer.

▶ **To add a local printer**

1. Log on to the local computer as Administrator or as a user who is a member of the Administrators group.
2. Click Start, click Control Panel, and then click Printers And Other Hardware.
3. Click Add A Printer to launch the Add Printer Wizard.

   Microsoft Windows XP Professional starts the Add Printer Wizard.
4. In the Welcome To The Add Printer Wizard page, click Next to continue.

   The Local Or Network Printer page appears.

   The Add Printer Wizard prompts you for the location of the printer. Because you are adding a printer on the computer at which you are sitting, this printer is referred to as a local printer.
5. Click Local Printer Attached To This Computer.
6. Ensure that the Automatically Detect And Install My Plug And Play Printer check box is cleared, and then click Next.

   The Add Printer Wizard then displays the Select A Printer Port page. The available port types depend on the installed network protocols. For this exercise, assume that the printer you are adding is directly attached to your computer and uses the LPT1 port.
7. Scroll through the Use The Following Port drop-down list box and review the selection of ports.
8. Verify that Use The Following Port is selected and that LPT1: (Recommended Printer Port) is selected.
9. Click Next.

   The Add Printer Wizard prompts you for the printer manufacturer and model. Assume that you will add an HP Color LaserJet 4550 PS printer.

Tip The printers are listed in alphabetical order. If you cannot find a printer name, make sure that you are looking in the correct location.

10. Under Manufacturers, choose HP.
11. Under Printers, select HP Color LaserJet 4550 PS.

> **Note** The selected driver is digitally signed to ensure reliability and to protect your system. Driver signing is covered in Chapter 11, "Installing, Managing, and Troubleshooting Hardware Devices and Drivers."

12. Click Next.

    The Name Your Printer page appears. In the Printer Name list box, Windows XP Professional automatically defaults to the printer name HP Color LaserJet 4550 PS. For this exercise, do not change this name.

    If other printers are already installed, the wizard also asks whether you want to make this the default printer.

13. If the Add Printer Wizard displays the Do You Want To Use This Printer As The Default Printer message, click Yes.

14. To accept the default printer name, click Next.

    The Printer Sharing page appears, prompting you for printer sharing information.

▶ **To share a printer**

1. In the Add Printer Wizard, on the Printer Sharing page, select Share Name.

    You can assign a shared printer name, even though you have already supplied a printer name.

> **Note** The shared printer name identifies a printer on the network and must conform to a naming convention. This shared name is different from the printer name that you entered previously. The printer name is a description that appears with the printer's icon in the Printers And Faxes folder and in the Active Directory service.

2. In the Share Name box, type **hpljc4550** and then click Next.

    The Add Printer Wizard displays the Location And Comment page.

> **Note** If your computer running Windows XP Professional is part of a domain, Microsoft Windows 2000 displays the values that you enter in the Location And Comment page when a user searches Active Directory for a printer. This information is optional, but it can help users locate the printer more easily.

3. In the Location text box, type **second floor west** and in the Comment text box type **mail room – room 2624**.

4. Click Next.

   The Add Printer Wizard displays the Print Test Page page.

   You can print a test page to confirm that your printer is set up properly. In this exercise you do not need a printer, so you will not print a test page. When you are actually setting up a printer, you should print a test page to confirm that the printer is working properly.

5. Under Do You Want To Print A Test Page, ensure that No is selected, and then click Next.

   The Add Printer Wizard displays the Completing The Add Printer Wizard page and shows a summary of your installation choices.

Note As you review the summary, you might want to change the information you entered, for example, to correct an error. To return to previous screens in the Add Printer Wizard to modify these settings, click Back.

6. When you are satisfied with your installation choices, click Finish.

   If necessary, Windows XP Professional displays the Files Needed dialog box, prompting you for the location of the Windows XP Professional distribution files.

7. If necessary, insert the *Microsoft Windows XP Professional* CD-ROM and wait for about 10 seconds.

8. If the Windows XP CD-ROM window appears, close it.

   If necessary, Windows XP Professional copies the printer files.

   Windows XP Professional has created an icon for the shared HP Color LaserJet 4550 PS printer in the Printers And Faxes window. Notice that an open hand is displayed on the printer icon, indicating that the printer is shared. The check mark just above the printer indicates that the printer is the default printer.

Exercise 2
Taking a Printer Offline and Printing a Test Document

In this exercise, you take the printer that you created offline. When a printer is offline, documents that you send to that printer are held on the computer while the printer is not available. This eliminates error messages about unavailable printers in later exercises. Windows XP Professional displays such error messages when it attempts to send documents to a printer that is not connected to the computer.

▶ **To take a printer offline**

1. In Control Panel, click Printers And Other Hardware.
2. In the Printers And Other Hardware window, click Printers And Faxes.
3. Right-click the HP Color LaserJet 4550 PS icon.
4. On the menu that appears, click Use Printer Offline.

   Windows XP Professional dims the icon and changes the status of the printer from Ready to Offline to show that the printer is not available.

▶ **To print a test document**

1. In the Printers And Faxes folder, double-click the HP Color LaserJet 4550 PS icon.

   Notice that the list of documents to be sent to the printer is empty.

2. Click Start, point to All Programs, point to Accessories, and then click Notepad.
3. In Microsoft Notepad, type any text that you want (for the purpose of creating a document to print).
4. Arrange Notepad and the HP Color LaserJet 4550 PS window so that you can see the contents of each.
5. In Notepad, on the File menu, click Print.

   The Print dialog box appears, allowing you to select the printer and print options.

Note Many programs running under Windows XP Professional use the same Print dialog box.

The Print dialog box shows the location and comment information that you entered when you created the printer. The status for the printer shows that it is currently offline. (You can also use this dialog box to search Active Directory for a printer.)

Notice that HP Color LaserJet 4550 PS is selected as the printer.

6. Click Print.

   Notepad briefly displays a message on your computer, stating that the document is printing. (On a fast computer, you might not be able to see this message.)

7. Close Notepad, and then click No when prompted to save changes to your document.

   In the HP Color LaserJet 4550 PS window, you see the document waiting to be sent to the printer. Windows XP Professional holds the document because you took the printer offline. Otherwise, Windows XP Professional would have sent the document to the printer.

8. Close the HP Color LaserJet 4550 PS window.

9. Close all open windows and log off the local computer.

Lab 7: Managing Printers

Objectives

After completing this lab, you will be able to

- Assign forms to paper trays
- Set up a separator page
- Assign printer permissions to a domain user

Note Completing this lab will help reinforce your learning from Chapter 7 of the textbook.

Before You Begin

In this lab, you'll perform three tasks that are part of managing printers. In Exercise 1, you'll assign forms to paper trays. In Exercise 2, you'll set up a separator page. In Exercise 3, you'll assign printer permissions to a domain user.

You must have set up a printer as described in Lab 6, "Installing a Network Printer," before you can perform this lab.

You must know your assigned student ID number.

You must have a lab partner assigned, and you must know his or her student ID number.

Estimated time to complete the lab: 20 minutes

Exercise 1
Assigning Forms to Paper Trays

In this exercise, you'll assign a paper type (form) to a paper tray so that when users print to a specified form, the print job is automatically routed to and adjusted for the correct tray.

▶ **To assign forms to a paper tray**

1. Log on to the local computer as Administrator or as a user who is a member of the Administrators group.
2. Click Start, click Control Panel, and then click Printers And Other Hardware.
3. Click Printers And Faxes.
4. Right-click the icon of your printer, and then click Properties.
5. In the HP Color LaserJet 4550 PS Properties dialog box, click the Device Settings tab.

    Some of the selections might be labeled Not Available or Not Installed because they depend on options that are not installed.

6. In the Device Settings tab of the HP Color LaserJet 4550 Properties dialog box, under Form To Tray Assignment, click the down arrow for Tray 2 and then select Legal.

    As a result of this selection, whenever a user prints on legal size paper, Microsoft Windows XP Professional will instruct the printer to use paper from Tray 2.

7. Click Apply, and leave the HP Color LaserJet 4550 Properties dialog box open for the next exercise.

Exercise 2
Setting Up Separator Pages

In this exercise, you'll set up a separator page to print between documents. You'll use the SYSPRINT.SEP separator page that ships with Windows XP Professional. This separator page includes the user's name and the date and time that the document was printed.

▶ **To set up a separator page**

1. In the HP Color LaserJet 4550 PS Properties dialog box, click the Advanced tab.
2. In the Advanced tab, click Separator Page.
3. In the Separator Page dialog box, click Browse.

   A second Separator Page dialog box appears, which lists the contents of the System32 folder. The System32 folder contains the separator pages that ship with Windows XP Professional. You can also use this dialog box to search in additional folders.

4. Select SYSPRINT.SEP, and then click Open.

   The Separator Page dialog box is displayed again, with the full path to the SYSPRINT.SEP separator page specified.

5. Click OK.

   Windows XP Professional is now set to print a separator page between print jobs.

   Leave the HP Color LaserJet 4550 PS Properties dialog box open for the next exercise.

Exercise 3
Assigning Printer Permissions to a Domain User

In this exercise, you'll assign printer permissions to a domain user (your lab partner).

▶ **To assign printer permissions**

1. In the HP Color LaserJet 4550 PS Properties dialog box, click the Security tab.
2. In the Security tab, click Advanced.

    The Advanced Security Settings For HP Color LaserJet 4550 PS dialog box appears.
3. Ensure that the Permissions tab is selected.
4. In the Permissions tab, click Add.

    The Select User, Computer, Or Group dialog box appears.
5. Click Advanced.

    The Enter Network Password dialog box appears.
6. In the User Name text box, type **Student$z$** (where z is your student ID number).
7. In the Password text box, type the password for Student$z$, and then click OK.
8. In the Select User, Computer, Or Group dialog box, under Common Queries, click the down arrow in the Name text box, and then select Is Exactly.
9. In the empty text box for Name, type **Student$p$** (where p is your lab partner's student ID number), and then click Find Now.

    Windows XP Professional should locate your lab partner's user account in the directory and display it at the bottom of the page.
10. Click OK.

    The Enter The Object Names To Select box now contains Student$p$.
11. Click OK to close the Select User, Computer, Or Group dialog box.

    The Permission Entry For HP Color LaserJet 4550 PS dialog box appears.
12. Select the Allow check box for Manage Printers.

    What permissions were automatically selected when you selected Manage Printers?

    _____

    _____

13. Click OK to close the Permission Entry dialog box.

    Notice that Student*p* is now listed in the Permission Entries box and has the Manage Printers permission assigned to it.

14. Click OK to close the Advanced Security Settings For HP Color LaserJet 4550 PS dialog box.
15. Click OK to close the HP Color LaserJet 4550 Properties dialog box.
16. Close the Printers And Faxes window and log off.

Lab 8: Managing Documents

Objectives

After completing this lab, you will be able to

- Set the notification for a document
- Increase the priority of a document in the print queue
- Cancel a document

Note Completing this lab will help reinforce your learning from Chapter 7 of the textbook.

Before You Begin

This lab uses the files you printed in Lab 6. If you have not completed Lab 6, you must print a document (to an offline printer) before you can complete this lab.

Estimated time to complete the lab: 15 minutes

Exercise 1
Setting the Notification for a Document

In this exercise, you'll set the notification for a document in the printer queue.

▶ **To set a notification**

1. Log on to your computer as Administrator.
2. Click Start, and then click Control Panel.
3. In the Control Panel window, click Printers And Other Hardware, and then click Printers And Faxes.
4. In the Printers And Faxes window, right-click the printer icon and verify that the Use Printer Online command is listed. (That command indicates the printer is currently offline.)
5. Click Open, and verify that a document is waiting to be printed.
6. In the Printer window, click the document to select it.
7. On the Document menu, click Properties.

   The Document Properties dialog box appears, with the General tab active.

   Which user is specified in the Notify text box?

   _____

   _____

8. In the Notify text box, type **Fred** (in place of the existing text), and then click Apply.

   You have now set the notification to go to user Fred.

   Leave the Printer window open for the next exercise.

Note You keep the printer offline to keep it from trying to print. This eliminates error messages in later exercises when documents are spooled.

Exercise 2
Increasing the Priority of a Document

In this exercise, you'll increase the priority of a document in the print queue and cancel a document.

▶ **To increase the priority of a document**

1. In the Document Properties dialog box, in the General tab, notice the default priority.

    What is the current priority? Is it the lowest or highest priority?

    _____

    _____

2. In the Priority box, move the slider to the right to increase the priority of the document to 38, and then click OK.

    Notice that nothing changes in the HP Color LaserJet 4550 PS – Use Printer Offline window.

▶ **To cancel a document**

1. In the HP Color LaserJet 4550 PS – Use Printer Offline window, select the document you want to cancel in the document list.

2. On the Document menu, click Cancel, and then click Yes to confirm.

    The Status column changes to Deleting as the document is being removed (but for a small document, the status changes so quickly that you will probably not see it). The document is removed from the document list.

3. Close the HP Color LaserJet 4550 PS – Use Printer Offline window, and then close the Printers And Faxes window.

4. Log off the computer.

Lab 9: Assigning NTFS Permissions

Objectives

After completing this lab, you will be able to

- Identify existing folder permissions
- Assign folder permissions
- Verify the assigned permissions
- Verify the inherited permissions

Note Completing this lab will help reinforce your learning from Chapter 8 of the textbook.

Before You Begin

To complete this lab, you'll need to know your student ID number. You'll also need a lab partner, or you'll need to know your lab partner's student ID number.

Estimated time to complete the lab: 20 minutes

Exercise 1
Determining the Default NTFS Folder Permissions

In this exercise, you'll determine the default NT file system (NTFS) permissions set on a folder.

▶ **To determine the default NTFS permissions on a folder**

1. Log on to the domain as DomUser$z$ (where z is your student ID number) with a password of **password**.
2. Click Start, right-click My Computer, and then click Explore.

Tip If you click the root of drive C, you may see a These Files Are Hidden message in the right pane instead of seeing files or folders in the right pane. If you get this message, click Show The Contents Of This Folder in the right pane.

3. Create the folder C:\Marketing, and then create the subfolder C:\Marketing\Presentations.

Tip To create the C:\Marketing folder, click Local Disk (C:) and then on the File menu, click New. Click Folder, type **Marketing** and then press ENTER. To create the folder C:\Marketing\Presentations, click Marketing and on the File menu, click New. Click Folder, type **Presentations** and then press ENTER.

4. Right-click the Presentations subfolder, and then click Properties.
5. In the Properties dialog box, click the Security tab.

   The Marketing Properties dialog box appears, with the Security tab active.

6. To determine if a user or group has special permissions set, click the user or group in the Group Or User Name box, and then in the Permissions For box, scroll down to Special and see if there is a check mark in the box.

   If there is a check mark in the Special check box, then the user or group you selected has special permissions set.

7. If any of the users or groups have special permissions, click the user or group, and then click Advanced to see which special permissions are set.

   What are the existing folder permissions?

   _____

   _____

   _____

   _____

   _____

   _____

   _____

8. Click OK to close the Properties dialog box for the folder.

Exercise 2
Testing NTFS Folder Permissions

In this exercise, you'll test NTFS folder default permissions as the creator of the folder and as a user.

▶ **To test the folder permissions for the Marketing folder**

1. In the Marketing folder, create a text document named DomUser$z$ (where z is your student ID number).

   Tip With the Marketing folder selected in the folder tree (the left pane), on the File menu, click New, and then click Text Document to create the text document.

   The text document can be empty for this exercise.
   Were you successful in creating the document? Why or why not?

   _____

   _____

   _____

2. Attempt to perform the following tasks for the file that you just created, and then record those tasks that you are able to complete.

   a. Open the document.

   b. Modify (and save the changes to) the document.

   c. Delete the document.

   Were you successful in completing all three tasks? Why or why not?

   _____

   _____

   _____

3. Re-create the text document named DomUser$z$ (where z is your student ID number), and type the following text in that document: **Have a nice day.** Then save the modified document.

4. Log off the domain.

5. Log on to the domain as DomUser$p$ (where p is your lab partner's student ID number) with a password of **password**.

Note In step 5, you should use your lab partner's domain user account to log on at your own computer, and your lab partner should use your domain user account to log on at his or her own computer.

6. Attempt to perform the following tasks on the DomUserz text document. Record whether you could perform the task, and why or why not.

   a. Open the file.

   Could you complete this task? Why or why not?

   _____

   _____

   _____

   b. Modify (and save the changes to) the file.

   Could you complete this task? Why or why not?

   _____

   _____

   _____

   c. Delete the file.

   Could you complete this task? Why or why not?

   _____

   _____

   _____

7. Log off the domain.

Exercise 3
Assigning NTFS Folder Permissions

In this exercise, you'll assign NTFS permissions for the Marketing folder. The permissions that you assign are to be based on the following criteria:

- All users should be able to read documents and files in the Presentations folder.
- All users should be able to create documents in the Presentations folder.
- All users should be able to modify the contents, properties, and permissions of the documents that they create in the Presentations folder.
- DomUser*p* (where *p* is your lab partner's student ID number) is responsible for maintaining the Presentations folder and should be able to modify and delete all files in the Presentations folder.

Based on what you learned in the previous exercises of this lab, what changes in permission assignments do you need to make to meet each of these four criteria? Why?

_____

_____

_____

_____

▶ **To assign NTFS permissions for a folder**

1. Log on to the domain as DomUser*z* (where *z* is your student ID number) with a password of **password.**
2. Click Start, right-click My Computer, and then click Explore.
3. Expand the Marketing folder.
4. Right-click the Marketing folder, and then click Properties.

   The Properties dialog box for the folder appears, with the General tab active.
5. In the Properties dialog box for the folder, click the Security tab.
6. In the Security tab, click Add.

   The Select Users, Computers, Or Groups dialog box appears.
7. In the Enter The Object Names To Select text box, type **DomUser*p*** (where *p* is your lab partner's student ID number), and then click Check Names.

   DomUser*p* should now appear in the Enter The Object Names To Select text box, indicating that it is a valid user account.

Lab 9: Assigning NTFS Permissions

8. Click OK to close the Select Users, Computers, Or Groups dialog box.

   DomUser*p* now appears in the Group Or User Names box in the Marketing Properties dialog box.

   What permissions are assigned to DomUser*p*?

   _____

   _____

9. Click Advanced.

   The Advanced Security Settings For Marketing dialog box appears, with DomUser*p* listed in the Permission Entries text box.

10. Ensure that DomUser*p* is selected, and then click Edit.

    The Permission Entry For Marketing dialog box appears, with DomUser*p* displayed in the Name text box.

11. In the Allow column, click Full Control.

    All the check boxes under Allow should now be selected.

12. Click OK to close the Permission Entry For Marketing dialog box.

    The Advanced Security Settings For Marketing dialog box appears.

13. Click OK to close the Advanced Security Settings For Marketing dialog box.

14. Click OK to close the Marketing Properties dialog box.

15. Log off the domain.

▶ **To test NTFS permissions for a folder**

1. Log on to the domain as DomUser*p* (where *p* is your lab partner's student ID number), and type **password** when prompted for the password.

2. Right-click My Computer, and then click Explore.

3. Expand Local Disk (C:), and then expand the Marketing folder.

4. Attempt to perform the following tasks on the DomUser*p* text document. Record whether you could perform the tasks, and why or why not.
   a. Open the file.
   b. Modify the file.
   c. Delete the file.

   _____

   _____

   _____

   _____

   _____

5. Close Windows Explorer and then log off Windows XP Professional.

Exercise 4
Verifying NTFS Folder Permissions Inheritance

In this exercise, you'll create a file in a subfolder and verify that NTFS permissions are inherited through a folder hierarchy.

▶ **To create a file with inherited NTFS permissions in the Presentations folder**

1. Log on to the domain as **DomUser*z*** (where *z* is your student ID number), right-click My Computer, and then click Explore.
2. Expand the Marketing folder, and then open the Presentations folder.
3. Create a text document named DomUser*z* in the Presentations folder.
4. Log off the domain.

▶ **To verify that the NTFS permissions for the Presentations folder were inherited while logged on as DomUser*p***

1. Log on to the domain as **DomUser*p*** (where *p* is your lab partner's student ID number) with a password of **password**.
2. Right-click My Computer, and then click Explore.
3. Expand the Marketing folder, and then open the Presentations folder.
4. Attempt to perform the following tasks on the DomUser*z* text document. Record whether you could perform the tasks, and why or why not.

    a. Open the file.
    b. Modify the file.
    c. Delete the file.

    _____
    _____
    _____
    _____

5. Log off the domain.

Lab 10: Managing NTFS Permissions

Objectives

After completing this lab, you will be able to

- Copy and move folders
- Determine how copying and moving folders affect ownership and NT file system (NTFS) permissions

Note Completing this lab will help reinforce your learning from Chapter 8 of the textbook.

Before You Begin

To complete this lab, you'll need to know your student ID number. You'll also need a lab partner, or you'll need to know your lab partner's student ID number.

Estimated time to complete the lab: 30 minutes

Exercise 1
Determining NTFS Folder Permissions

In this exercise, you'll determine the default NTFS permissions set on a folder created by a domain user.

▶ **To create a folder while logged on as a domain user**

1. Log on to the domain as **DomUser**z (where *z* is your student ID number) with a password of **password**.
2. Click Start, right-click My Computer, and then click Explore.
3. In the root folder of drive C, create a folder named Temp*z*.

   Who is the owner of Temp*z*? Why?

> **Note** If you cannot remember how to determine the owner of a folder or how to determine the permissions set on a folder, review the steps in Lab 9 in this manual.

_____

_____

What are the permissions set on Temp*z*?

_____

_____

_____

_____

_____

_____

4. Log off the domain.

Exercise 2
Creating Folders and Assigning NTFS Folder Permissions

In this exercise, you'll log on as the local Administrator, create some folders, and assign NTFS permissions to them.

▶ **To create folders while logged on as a local Administrator**

1. Log on to the computer (not the domain) as Administrator with a password of **password**.
2. In the root folder of drive C, create the folders TempA and TempB.

   Who is the owner of the TempA and TempB folders?

   _____

   What are the permissions set on the TempA and TempB folders?

   _____

   _____

   _____

   _____

   _____

3. In the Security tab of the TempA Properties dialog box, click Advanced to access the Advanced Security Settings For TempA dialog box and clear the Inherit From Parent The Permission Entries That Apply To Child Objects check box.

   A Security message box appears, asking what you want to do. You have the following three choices:

   - Copy the permission entries that were previously applied from the parent to this object
   - Remove the permission entries that were previously applied from the parent and keep only those permissions explicitly defined here
   - Cancel to cancel operation and close the message box

4. Click Remove to remove all permissions.
5. In the Advanced Security Settings For TempA dialog box, click Add.
6. In the Select Users, Computers, Or Groups dialog box, in the Enter The Object Name To Select text box, type **Administrators** and then click OK.
7. In the Enter Network Password dialog box, in the User Name text box, type **Student$z$** (where z is your student ID number), and in the Password text box, type **password**.
8. Click OK.

    A Select Users, Computers, Or Groups message box appears, indicating that the Administrators group was not found.

    Why is the Administrators group not found? (For a hint, close the message box and look at the From This Location text box in the Advanced Security Settings for TempA dialog box.)

    _____

    _____

    _____

9. In the Advanced Security Settings for TempA dialog box, in the Enter The Object Name To Select text box, type **Domain Admins** and then click OK.
10. In the Permission Entry For TempA dialog box, click Full Control to assign the Domain Admins group the Full Control permission for the TempA folder, and then click OK.
11. Click OK to close the Advanced Security Settings For TempA dialog box.
12. In the TempA Properties dialog box, click Add.
13. In the Select Users, Computers, Or Groups dialog box, in the Enter The Object Names To Select text box, type **DomUser$p$** (where p is your lab partner's student ID number), and then click OK.
14. In the TempA Properties dialog box, ensure that Read & Execute, List Folder Contents, and Read are the only permissions selected for DomUser$p$.
15. In the TempA Properties dialog box, click Add.
16. In the Select Users, Computers, Or Groups dialog box, in the Enter The Object Names To Select text box, type **DomUser$z$** and then click OK.
17. Click Full Control to assign this permission to the DomUser$z$ user.
18. Click OK to close the TempA Properties dialog box.
19. Log off the computer.

Exercise 3
Copying Folders Within an NTFS Volume

In this exercise, you'll log on as a domain user, copy a folder, and determine how the ownership and NTFS permissions change when you copy a folder.

▶ **To copy a folder to another folder within a Microsoft Windows XP Professional NTFS volume**

1. Log on to the domain as **DomUser*z*** (where *z* is your student ID number).
2. Click Start, right-click My Computer, and then click Explore.
3. Copy the folder C:\TempA to C:\Temp*z* by selecting C:\TempA, holding down CTRL, and then dragging C:\TempA to C:\Temp*z*.

Note Because this is a copy, C:\TempA and C:\Temp*z*\TempA should both exist.

4. Select C:\Temp*z*\TempA, and then compare the permissions and ownership with C:\TempA.

   Who is the owner of C:\Temp*z*\TempA and what are the permissions? Why?

   _____
   _____
   _____
   _____
   _____

5. Delete C:\Temp*z*\TempA.

Exercise 4
Moving Folders Within an NTFS Volume

In this exercise, while logged on as a domain user, you'll move a folder and determine how the ownership and NTFS permissions change when you move a folder.

▶ **To move a folder within an NTFS volume**

1. While logged on to the domain as **DomUser***z* (where *z* is your student ID number), in Windows Explorer select C:\TempA, and then drag it to C:\Temp*z*.

   Note You do not hold down CTRL this time because you want to move the folder, not copy it.

   What happens to the permissions and ownership for C:\Temp*z*\TempA? Why?

   _____

   _____

   _____

2. Close all windows and log off the domain.

Lab 11: Managing Shared Folders

Objectives

After completing this lab, you will be able to

- Share folders
- Add and remove groups for shared folder permissions
- Assign shared folder permissions
- Connect to a shared folder
- Understand how NT file system (NTFS) permissions and shared folder permissions combine

Note Completing this lab will help reinforce your learning from Chapter 9 of the textbook.

Before You Begin

You'll need to know your student ID number to log on to the domain as Student*z*, where *z* is your student ID number. Student*z* is a member of the Domain Admins group. You'll also be logging on to the domain as DomUser*z* (where *z* is your student ID number). DomUser*z* is a member of the Domain Users group.

You'll also need to know the domain number, and your lab partner's student ID number and computer number.

Estimated time to complete the lab: 30 minutes

Exercise 1
Creating a Shared Folder

In this exercise, you'll determine the default NTFS permissions set on a folder created by a domain user.

▶ **To share a folder**

1. Log on to the Corp*y* domain as **Student*z*** (where *y* is the domain number and *z* is your student ID number) with a password of **password**.
2. Click Start, right-click My Computer, and then click Explore.
3. In the root folder of drive C, create a folder named Student*z*.
4. Right-click the Student*z* folder, and then click Sharing And Security.

   The Student*z* Properties dialog box appears, with the Sharing tab active.
5. In the Sharing tab, click Share This Folder.

   The Share Name value defaults to the name of the folder.
6. In the Comment text box, type **Student*z*'s shared files** and then click OK.

   A hand icon appears under the Student*z* folder, indicating that it is a shared folder.

Exercise 2
Assigning Shared Folder Permissions

In this exercise, you'll determine the current permissions for a shared folder and assign shared folder permissions to groups in your domain.

▶ **To view folder permissions**

1. Click Start, right-click My Computer, and then click Explore.
2. Right-click the Studentz folder, and then click Sharing And Security.

    The Studentz Properties dialog box appears, with the Sharing tab active.

3. Click Permissions.

    The Permissions For Studentz dialog box appears. The default permissions are set for the Everyone group to have Full Control.

▶ **To remove shared folder permissions from a group**

1. In the Permissions For Studentz dialog box, in the Group Or User Names list box, verify that Everyone is selected.
2. Click Remove.

    Microsoft Windows XP Professional removes the Everyone group from the list box.

▶ **To assign a group shared folder permissions**

1. In the Permissions For Studentz dialog box, click Add.

    The Select Users, Computers, Or Groups dialog box appears.

2. In the Enter The Object Names To Select text box, type **Domain Users**.
3. Click Check Names.

    Windows XP Professional verifies that the Domain Users group is valid.

4. Click OK.

    Windows XP Professional closes the Select Users, Computers, Or Groups dialog box and displays the Permissions For Studentz dialog box.

    Domain Users is now listed in the Group Or User Names list box and has the Read permission assigned to it.

    Tip If you wanted to change the assigned permissions, you would select the appropriate check box. The selections are Change and Full Control.

5. Click OK to close the Permissions For Studentz dialog box.
6. Click OK to close the Studentz Properties dialog box.
7. Close all windows and log off the domain.

Exercise 3
Connecting to a Shared Folder Using the Run Command

In this exercise, you'll connect to a shared folder on your lab partner's computer.

Note Before you begin Exercise 3, ensure that your lab partner has completed Exercises 1 and 2.

▶ **To connect to a shared folder using the Run command**

1. Log on to the Corp*y* domain as **DomUser*z*** (where *y* is the domain number and *z* is your student ID number) with a password of **password**.
2. Click Start, and then click Run.
3. In the Open text box, type **\\Computer*p*** (where *p* is your lab partner's computer number), and then click OK.

   Windows XP Professional displays the Computer*p* window.
4. Double-click the Student*p* folder icon to confirm that you can access its contents.
5. Create a text document in the Student*p* folder on your lab partner's computer.

   Were you able to create a text document? Why or why not?

   _____

   _____

   _____

6. Close all windows and log off the domain.

Exercise 4
Removing and Assigning Shared Folder Permissions

In this exercise, you'll remove shared folder permissions from a group and assign shared folder permissions to a group. Then you'll connect to the share to verify that the shared folder permissions you assigned are working.

▶ **To change shared folder permissions**

1. Log on to the Corp*y* domain as **Student*z*** (where *y* is the domain number and *z* is your student ID number) with a password of **password**.
2. Click Start, right-click My Computer, and then click Explore.
3. Right-click the Student*z* folder icon, and then click Sharing And Security.

    The Student*z* Properties dialog box appears, with the Sharing tab active.
4. Click Permissions.
5. In the Permissions For Student*z* dialog box, verify that Domain Users is selected.
6. Clear the Allow check box next to Read.

    You have just removed shared folder permission from a group.
7. Select the Allow check box next to Full Control.

    You have just assigned shared folder permissions to a group.
8. Click OK.
9. Click OK to close the Student*z* Properties dialog box.
10. Close all windows and log off the domain.

▶ **To test shared folder permissions**

Note Before you begin this procedure, ensure that your lab partner has completed the first procedure in Exercise 4.

1. Log on to the Corp*y* domain as **DomUser*z*** (where *y* is the domain number and *z* is your student ID number) with a password of **password**.
2. Click Start, and then click Run.
3. In the Open text box, type **\\Computer*p*** (where *p* is your lab partner's computer number), and then click OK.
4. Double-click the Student*p* folder icon to confirm that you can access its contents.
5. Attempt to create a text document in the Student*p* folder on your lab partner's computer.

    You should now be able to create a text document.
6. Close all windows and log off the domain.

Exercise 5
Checking and Assigning NTFS Permissions

In this exercise, you'll assign new NTFS permissions and test how they combine with the existing Full Control shared folder permissions.

▶ **To assign NTFS permissions**

1. Log on to the Corp*y* domain as **Student*z*** (where *y* is the domain number and *z* is your student ID number) with a password of **password**.
2. Click Start, right-click My Computer, and then click Explore.
3. Right-click C:\Student*z* on your local computer, and then click Properties.
4. In the Student*z* Properties dialog box, click the Security tab.
5. Under Group Or User Names, click Users (Computer*z*\Users).

   Notice that the Users group has the Read & Execute, List Folder Contents, Read and Special Permissions NTFS permissions assigned by default.

6. Click Advanced.

   The Advanced Security Settings For Student*z* dialog box appears.

7. Clear the check box in front of Inherit From Parent The Permission Entries That Apply To Child Objects.

   A Security message box appears, asking if you want to copy or remove the permission entries that were previously applied from the parent.

8. Click Copy to keep the permission entries previously applied from the parent.
9. In the Advanced Security Settings For Student*z* dialog box, click Users (Computer*z*\Users) (Special Permissions), and then click Edit.

   Notice that the Users group has the Create Files/Write Data and the Create Folders/Append Data special NTFS permissions assigned.

10. Clear the Allow check box for the Create Files/Write Data and the Create Folders/Append Data special NTFS permissions.
11. Click OK to apply the changes and close the Permissions Entry For Student*z* dialog box.
12. Click OK to close the Advanced Security Settings For Student*z* dialog box.
13. Click Apply, and then click OK to close the Student*z* Properties dialog box.
14. Close all open windows and log off the domain.

Lab 11: Managing Shared Folders 73

▶ **To test the effective permissions**

Note You cannot continue with this exercise until your lab partner has completed the previous procedure.

1. Log on to the Corp*y* domain as **DomUser*z*** (where *y* is the domain number and *z* is your student ID number) with a password of **password**.
2. Click Start, and then click Run.
3. In the Open text box, type **\\Computer*p*** (where *p* is your lab partner's computer number), and then click OK.
4. Double-click the Student*p* folder icon (where *p* is your lab partner's student ID number).
5. Create a text document in the Student*p* folder on your partner's computer.

   Were you able to create a text document? Why or why not?

   _____

   _____

   _____

   _____

   _____

6. Close all windows and log off the domain.

Exercise 6
Connecting to a Shared Folder Using the Add Network Place Wizard

In this exercise, you'll use the Add Network Place Wizard to connect to a shared folder on your partner's computer.

▶ **To connect to a shared folder using the Add Network Place Wizard**

1. Log on to the Corp$y$ domain as **Student$z$** (where y is the domain number and z is your student ID number) with a password of **password**.
2. Click Start, and then click Control Panel.
3. Click Network And Internet Connections.
4. In the Network And Internet Connections window, under See Also, click My Network Places.
5. In My Network Places, under Network Tasks, click Add A Network Place.
6. In the Welcome To The Add Network Place Wizard page, click Next.
7. In the Where Do You Want To Create This Network Place page, click Next to accept the default of Choose Another Network Location.
8. In the What Is The Address Of This Network Place page, in the Internet Or Network Address text box, type **\\Computer$p$\Student$p$** (where p is your lab partner's student ID number and computer number), and then click Next.
9. In the What Do You Want To Name This Place page, click Next to accept the default setting in the Type A Name For This Network Place text box.
10. In the Completing The Add Network Place Wizard page, click Finish.

    The Student$p$ On Computer$p$ window appears, indicating your connection is made.
11. Close all windows and log off the domain.

Lab 12: Configuring Automatic Updates and the Remote Assistance Feature

Objectives

After completing this lab, you will be able to

- Configure Automatic Updates (AU)
- Configure the Remote Assistance feature
- Use Remote Desktop Connection to connect to a remote computer

Note Completing this lab will help reinforce your learning from Chapter 10 of the textbook.

Before You Begin

You'll need to know your student ID number to log on to the domain as Student$z$, where z is your student ID number. Student$z$ is a member of the Domain Admins group.

You'll also need to know the domain number, and you'll need to have an assigned lab partner.

Estimated time to complete the lab: 20 minutes

Exercise 1
Configuring Automatic Updates

In this exercise, you'll configure AU.

▶ **To configure automatic updates**

1. Log on to the Corp*y* domain as **Student***z* (where *y* is the domain number and *z* is your student ID number) with a password of **password**.
2. Click Start, and then click Control Panel.
3. Click Performance And Maintenance, and then click System.
4. In the System Properties dialog box, click Automatic Updates.
5. In the Automatic Updates tab, under Notification Settings, click Notify Me Before Downloading Any Updates And Notify Me Again Before Installing Them On My Computer.

Leave the System Properties dialog box open for the next exercise.

Exercise 2
Configuring the Remote Assistance Feature

In this exercise, you'll configure the Remote Assistance feature on your computer.

▶ **To configure the Remote Assistance feature**

1. In the System Properties dialog box, click Remote.

    The Remote tab is active.

2. Under Remote Assistance, click Advanced.

    The Remote Assistance Settings dialog box appears.

3. Under Remote Control, clear the Allow This Computer To Be Controlled Remotely check box.

    What would happen if the Allow This Computer To Be Controlled Remotely check box were selected?

    _____

4. Under Invitations, in the first pull-down text box for Set The Maximum Amount Of Time Invitations Can Remain Open, select 14. In the second pull-down text box, ensure that Days is selected, so that invitations can remain open for 14 days.

5. Click OK to close the Remote Assistance Settings dialog box.

6. In the Remote tab, in the System Properties dialog box, under Remote Desktop, select Allow Users To Connect Remotely To This Computer.

    A Remote Sessions message box appears. What two warnings does it give?

    _____

    _____

7. Click OK to close the Remote Sessions message box.

8. In the Remote tab, in the System Properties dialog box, click Select Remote Users.

    A Remote Users Desktop dialog box appears.

    Notice, just above the Add button, the indication that Studentz already has access to connect to this computer remotely.

9. Click Cancel to close the Remote Desktop Users dialog box.
10. Click Apply, and then click OK to close the System Properties dialog box.

    You have now configured remote access to your computer.

Exercise 3
Connecting to a Remote Computer

In this exercise, you'll log on to your lab partner's computer. Then you'll use Remote Desktop Connection to make a remote connection to your computer.

When both you and your partner have completed Exercise 2, you should change seats. One of you will complete Exercise 3. When the first partner completes Exercise 3, if there is time, the other partner should also complete Exercise 3.

▶ **To connect to a remote computer**

1. At your lab partner's computer, log on to the Corp*y* domain as **Student*z*** (where *y* is the domain number and *z* is your student ID number) with a password of **password**.

2. Click Start, point to All Programs, point to Accessories, point to Communications, and then click Remote Desktop Connection.

    The Remote Desktop Connection dialog box appears.

3. In the Computer text box, type **Computer*z*** (where *z* is your student ID number).

4. Click Connect.

    A Log On To Windows dialog box appears.

5. Log on to the Corp*y* domain as Student*z*.

    Were you able to remotely connect to your computer?

    _____

    If you look at the monitor on your own computer, Computer*z*, where your partner is currently sitting, notice that it is now locked.

6. To close the remote connection, log off the domain.

7. Log off the domain at your partner's computer.

Lab 13: Installing Fax Services

Objectives

After completing this lab, you will be able to

- Use the Windows Component Wizard
- Install Fax Services

Note Completing this lab will help reinforce your learning from Chapter 11 of the textbook.

Estimated time to complete the lab: 15 minutes

Exercise 1
Using the Windows Components Wizard to Install Fax Services

In this exercise, you'll install and configure Fax Services.

▶ **To configure Fax Services**

1. Log on to the local computer as **Administrator** with a password of **password**.
2. Click Start, click Control Panel, and then click Add Or Remove Programs.
3. In the Add Or Remove Programs window, click Add/Remove Windows Components.

    The Windows Components Wizard starts.

4. In the Windows Components Wizard, click the check box in front of Fax Services (there should now be a check mark in the check box indicating that it is selected), and then click Next.

    The Windows Components Wizard displays the Configuring Components page while the wizard examines the components, copies the necessary files, and configures Fax Services.

5. When the Windows Components Wizard displays the Completing The Windows Components Wizard page, read the page, and then click Finish.
6. Close the Add Or Remove Programs window.
7. Close Control Panel and log off.

Lab 14: Auditing Resources and Events

Objectives

After completing this lab, you will be able to

- Set up an audit policy
- Enable auditing on a folder
- Use Event Viewer to look at the security log
- Use the Filter command to locate specific events in the security log

Note Completing this lab will help reinforce your learning from Chapter 12 of the textbook.

Before You Begin

Before you start this lab, you'll need to know your student ID number, your lab partner's student ID number, and the domain number.

Estimated time to complete the lab: 30 minutes

Exercise 1
Setting Up an Audit Policy

In this exercise, you'll use the Group Policy snap-in to set up an audit policy for a local computer.

▶ **To set up an audit policy**

1. Log on to the local computer as **Administrator** with a password of **password**.
2. Click Start, click Run, and in the Open text box, type **mmc** and then click OK.
3. In the Console1 window, on the File menu, click Add/Remove Snap-In.
4. In the Add/Remove Snap-In dialog box, click Add.
5. In the Add Standalone Snap-In dialog box, select Group Policy, and then click Add.
6. In the Select Group Policy Object dialog box, ensure that the Group Policy Object text box says Local Computer, and then click Finish.
7. In the Add Standalone Snap-In dialog box, click Close.

    In the Add/Remove Snap-In dialog box, notice that it says Local Computer Policy, even though you added Group Policy. Group Policy for the local computer is referred to as Local Computer Policy.

8. In the Add/Remove Snap-In dialog box, click OK.
9. In the console tree of the Local Computer Policy Snap-In, double-click Local Computer Policy.
10. Double-click Computer Configuration, then Windows Settings, then Security Settings, and then Local Policies.
11. Double-click Security Settings, and then double-click Local Policies.
12. Click Audit Policy.

    The console displays the current audit policy settings in the details pane of the Local Computer Policy window.

13. In the details pane, double-click Audit Logon Events.
14. In the Audit Logon Events Properties dialog box, select Success, select Failure, and then click OK.
15. In the details pane, double-click Audit Object Access.
16. In the Audit Object Access Properties dialog box, select Success, select Failure, and then click OK.
17. On the File menu, click Exit.

18. In the Microsoft Management Console message box, click Yes to save the console settings for Console1.
19. In the Save As dialog box, in the File Name text box, type **Local Group Policy** and then click Save.
20. Restart your computer to make the changes take effect immediately.

Exercise 2
Setting Up Auditing on a Folder

In this exercise, you'll set up auditing for a folder.

▶ **To enable auditing for a folder**

1. Log on to the local computer as **Administrator** with a password of **password**.
2. In Windows Explorer, create a folder named Auditing in the root folder of your system disk (for example, C:\Auditing).
3. Create a text document named AuditTest in the Auditing folder (for example, C:\Auditing\AuditTest).
4. Right-click the Auditing folder, and then click Properties.
5. In the Auditing Properties dialog box, click the Security tab, and then click Advanced.
6. In the Advanced Security Settings For Auditing dialog box, click Auditing.
7. In the Auditing tab, click Add.
8. In the Select User, Computer, Or Group dialog box, in the Name text box, type **Everyone** and then click OK.
9. In the Enter Network Password dialog box, in the User Name text box, type **Student$z$** (where z is your student ID number), and in the Password dialog box, type **password** and then click OK.
10. In the Auditing Entry For Auditing dialog box, select the Successful and Failed check boxes for each of the following events:
    - Create Files/Write Data
    - Delete
    - Change Permissions
    - Take Ownership
11. Click OK to close the Auditing Entry For Auditing dialog box.

    The Everyone group appears in the Advanced Security Settings For Auditing dialog box.
12. Click OK to apply your changes and close the Advanced Security Settings For Auditing dialog box.

    Leave the Auditing Properties dialog box open for the next procedure.

Exercise 3
Sharing a Folder and Verifying the Shared Folder and NTFS Permissions

In this exercise, you'll share a folder, set shared folder permissions, and verify the NT file system (NTFS) permissions.

▶ **To share the Auditing folder**

1. In the Auditing Properties dialog box, click Sharing.
2. In the Sharing tab, select Share This Folder.
3. Click Permissions.

   What are the current shared folder permissions for the Auditing folder?

   _____

4. In the Permissions For Everyone box, clear all the check boxes except the Allow check box for Read, and then click OK.
5. In the Auditing Properties dialog box, click Apply to accept the default share name of Auditing.

▶ **To verify file permissions**

1. In the Auditing Properties dialog box, click Security.
2. In the Security tab of the Auditing Properties dialog box, click Advanced.
3. In the Permissions tab, select Users (*Computer_name*\Users) Read&Execute, and then click Edit.
4. Verify that the Allow permissions for the folder are Traverse Folder/Execute File, List Folder/Read Data, Read Attributes, Read Extended Attributes, and Read Permissions.
5. Click Cancel to close the Permission Entry For Auditing dialog box.
6. Click Cancel to close the Advanced Security Settings For Auditing dialog box.
7. Click Cancel to close the Auditing Properties dialog box.
8. Close Windows Explorer and log off the local computer.

Exercise 4
Testing the Audit Policy

Before beginning Exercise 4, you and your lab partner must have completed Exercise 3. In Exercise 4, your lab partner will attempt to access and modify the AuditTest file on your computer to create entries in the security log for your computer.

▶ **To test the audit policy**

1. Log on to the Corp*y* domain as **Student*z*** (where *z* is your student ID number and *y* is the domain number) with a password of **password**.
2. Click Start, and then click Run.
3. In the Open text box, type **\\Computer*p*** (where *p* is your lab partner's student ID number), and then click OK.
4. Double-click Auditing.
5. Double-click AuditTest.
6. In Microsoft Notepad, type the following text: **Student*z* modified this file.**
7. On the File menu, click Save.

    A message box indicates that you are not able to save the file.

    Why are you unable to save the modified file?

    _____

    _____

    _____

8. Click OK to close the message box.
9. Click Cancel to close the Save As dialog box.
10. On the File menu, click Exit.
11. When prompted to save changes, click No, and then log off the domain.

Exercise 5
Viewing the Security Log

Before beginning Exercise 5, you and your lab partner must have completed Exercise 4. In Exercise 5, you'll view the security log on your computer.

▶ **To view and filter the security log**

1. Log on to the local computer as **Administrator** with a password of **password**.

2. Click Start, click Control Panel, click Performance And Maintenance, click Administrative Tools, and then double-click the Event Viewer shortcut.

3. In the console tree, click the security log and view the contents. As you scroll through the log, double-click each of the Failure Audit events until you locate the one for Student*p* (where *p* is your lab partner's student ID number) when Student*p* tried to access C:\Auditing\.

4. On the View menu, click Filter.

5. In the Security Properties dialog box, in the User text box, type **Student*p*** and then click OK.

6. Double-click each of the events and notice that all of them apply to Student*p*.

7. Close Event Viewer and log off the local computer.

Lab 15: Configuring Internet Options

Objectives

After completing this lab, you will be able to

- Configure Internet security using the Internet Options in Microsoft Windows XP Professional
- Use the Microsoft Profile Assistant to create an Internet profile

Note Completing this lab will help reinforce your learning from Chapter 13 of the textbook.

Estimated time to complete the lab: 15 minutes

Exercise 1
Configuring Internet Options

In this exercise, you'll use Internet Options to configure Internet security on your computer running Windows XP Professional.

▶ **To configure Internet Options**

1. Log on to the local computer as **Administrator** with a password of **password**.
2. Click Start, and then click Control Panel.
3. Click Network And Internet Connections, and then click Internet Options.

   The Internet Properties dialog box appears, with the General tab selected.

   What is your home page?

   _____

4. Under Temporary Internet Files, click Settings.
5. Under Check For Newer Versions Of Stored Pages, select Every Visit To The Page.
6. Under Temporary Internet Files Folder, click View Files.

   Are any files listed?

   _____

7. On the File menu, click Close to close the Temporary Internet Files window.
8. Click OK to close the Settings dialog box.
9. Under History, set Days To Keep Pages In History to **7**.
10. Click Apply.
11. Click Content.
12. Under Personal Information, click My Profile.

    The Address Book – Choose Profile dialog box appears.

    What is the purpose of My Profile?

    _____

    _____

13. Ensure that Create A New Entry In The Address Book To Represent Your Profile is selected, and then click OK.

    The Properties dialog box appears.

14. Type your first, middle, and last names in the appropriate text boxes.

    Notice that the Display text box is automatically filled in for you.

15. In the E-mail Addresses text box, type your e-mail address, and then click Add.

    Notice that your e-mail address is now listed as the (Default E-Mail) address.

16. Click OK to close the *display* Properties dialog box (where *display* is the name listed in the Display text box).

17. Click OK to close the Internet Properties dialog box.

18. On the File menu, click Close to close the Network And Internet Connections dialog box.

19. Log off the computer.

Lab 16: Using the Compressed Folders Feature

Objectives

After completing this lab, you will be able to

- Create a compressed folder using the Compressed Folders feature
- Drag and drop files into a compressed folder created with the Compressed Folders feature

Note Completing this lab will help reinforce your learning from Chapter 14 of the textbook.

Before You Begin

Before you start this lab, you'll need to know your student ID number.

Estimated time to complete the lab: 15 minutes

Exercise 1
Creating a Compressed Folder by Using the Compressed Folders Feature

In this exercise, you'll use the new Compressed Folders feature in Microsoft Windows XP Professional to create a compressed folder.

▶ **To create a compressed folder by using the Compressed Folders feature**

1. Log on to the domain as **Studentz** (where z is your student ID number).
2. Click Start, right-click My Computer, and then click Explore.
3. In the Folders pane, click Local Disk (C:) to select it, and then expand it.
4. On the File menu, point to New, and then click Compressed (Zipped) Folder.

    Windows XP Professional creates a new folder named New Compressed (Zipped) Folder in the details pane. Notice it is selected so that you can rename the folder.

5. Type **Studentz's Compressed Folder** to rename the folder.
6. Minimize Windows Explorer.

Exercise 2
Creating a File and Dragging and Dropping It into a Compressed Folder

In this exercise, you'll use Microsoft WordPad to create a file, you'll attempt to save it into your compressed folder, and finally, you'll drag and drop a file into the compressed folder you created with the Compressed Folders feature.

▶ **To create and save a file using WordPad**

1. Click Start, point to All Programs, point to Accessories, and then click WordPad.
2. In WordPad, type **I am creating a document to test how the new Compressed Folders feature works.**
3. On the File menu, click Save.

    The Save As dialog box appears.

4. In the Save In list box, click the drop-down arrow to display locations to save the file.
5. Click Local Disk (C:) to display the folders on drive C in which you can save your file.

    Why is Student$z$'s Compressed Folder not listed among the folders in which you can save your file?

    _____

    _____

6. In the File Name text box, type **Student$z$** (where z is your student ID number), and then click Save to save the file with the name Student$z$ in the root folder of drive C.
7. On the File menu, click Exit to close WordPad.

▶ **To drag and drop a file into a compressed folder created by using the Compressed Folders feature**

1. In the Taskbar, click Local Disk (C:) to restore Windows Explorer.
2. Click the Student$z$ file and, while holding down the mouse button, drag and drop the file into Student$z$'s Compressed Folder (where z is your student ID number).

3. Double-click Studentz's Compressed Folder to view the contents of the folder.
4. Double-click Studentz.

   What happened? What does that demonstrate?

   _____

   _____

   _____

5. On the File menu, click Exit to close WordPad.
6. Log off the domain.

Lab 17: Creating Remote Shared Folders

Objectives

After completing this lab, you will be able to

- Create a custom Microsoft Management Console (MMC) console containing the Shared Folders snap-in and pointing to a remote computer
- Use the Create Shared Folder Wizard to create and share a folder on a remote computer
- Use the Computer Management snap-in to view open files on your computer and to disconnect all open files
- Use the Computer Management snap-in to view any open sessions on your computer

Note Completing this lab will help reinforce your learning from Chapter 15 of the textbook.

Before You Begin

Before you start this lab, you'll need to know your student ID number, your lab partner's student ID number, and the Corpy domain number.

Estimated time to complete the lab: 30 minutes

Exercise 1
Creating and Sharing a Folder on a Remote Computer

In this exercise, you'll create a custom MMC console containing the Shared Folders snap-in and pointing to a remote computer. You'll use this custom MMC console to create and share a folder on a remote computer (your lab partner's computer).

▶ **To create a custom MMC console containing the Shared Folders snap-in pointing to a remote computer**

1. Log on to the domain as Student$z$ (where z is your student ID number).
2. Click Start, and then click Run.
3. In the Open text box, type **mmc** and then click OK.

   The Microsoft Management Console appears, with a blank console displayed.
4. On the File menu, click Add/Remove Snap-In.
5. In the Add/Remove Snap-In dialog box, click Add.

   The Add Standalone Snap-In dialog box appears.
6. Select Shared Folders, and then click Add.

   The Shared Folders dialog box appears.
7. In the Shared Folders dialog box, select Another Computer, and then select the text box following Another Computer and type **Computer$p$** (where p is your partner's student ID number).
8. Click Finish.
9. Click Close to close the Add Standalone Snap-In dialog box.
10. Click OK to close the Add/Remove Snap-In dialog box.

    Leave Console1 (the custom MMC console you just created) open for the next procedure.

▶ **To create a shared folder on a remote computer**

1. In the console tree (left pane) of Console1, expand Shared Folders.
2. In the console tree of Console1, right-click Shares, and then click New File Share.

   The Create Shared Folder Wizard appears.
3. In the Folder To Share text box, type **C:\Student$z$Remote** (where z is your student ID number).
4. In the Share Name text box, type **Student$z$Remote**.

5. In the Share Description text box, type **Studentz's Remote Shared Folder** and then click Next.

   The Create Shared Folder dialog box appears, indicating that the system could not find the folder and asking if you would like the system to create the folder.

6. Click Yes.

7. Select Customize Share And Folder Permissions, and then click Custom.

   What are the current share permissions?

   _____

Tip Using the Customize Permissions dialog box, you can change the share permissions. If you click the Security tab, you can also customize the NTFS permissions.

8. Click Cancel to close the Customize Permissions dialog box.
9. Click Finish.

   A Create Shared Folder dialog box appears, indicating that the folder has been created and shared successfully for Microsoft Windows clients. You are also prompted to create another folder.

10. Click No to close the dialog box and the Create Shared Folder Wizard.
11. In the console tree (left pane) of Console1, click Shares, and then verify that StudentzRemote is listed in the details pane.
12. In Console1, on the File menu, click Exit.

    A Microsoft Management Console message box appears, asking you if you want to save the console settings for Console1.

13. Click Yes.
14. In the File Name text box, type **Shared Folders on Computer$p$** (where p is your lab partner's student ID number).
15. Click Save.

Exercise 2
Creating a File in a Remote Shared Folder

In this exercise, you'll use Microsoft WordPad to create a file and to save it in the remote shared folder, Student$z$Remote.

▶ **To create and save a file, using WordPad**

1. Click Start, point to All Programs, point to Accessories, and then click WordPad.
2. In WordPad, type **I am creating a document to have a file in my Student$z$Remote folder** (where z is your student ID number).
3. On the File menu, click Save.

    The Save As dialog box appears.
4. If the Save In list box displays Student$z$Remote on Computer$p$ (where z is your student ID number and p is your lab partner's student ID number), go to step 9; otherwise, go to step 5.
5. Click the down arrow at the end of the text box to display locations to save the file.
6. Double-click My Network Places, double-click Entire Network, and then double-click Microsoft Windows Network.
7. Double-click Corp$y$ (where y is the domain number).
8. Double-click Computer$p$.
9. Double-click Student$z$Remote to select the Student$z$Remote shared folder.
10. In the File Name text box, type **Student$z$Remote File**, and then click Save.

    This saves the Student$z$Remote File in the Student$z$Remote folder on drive C of your lab partner's computer.
11. On the File menu, click Exit to close WordPad.

Exercise 3
Connecting to a Shared Folder on a Remote Computer and Opening a File

In this exercise, you'll connect to a share on your partner's computer and open a file in the share.

Note Before beginning this exercise, both you and your lab partner must have completed Exercise 2.

▶ **To connect to a shared folder on your partner's computer**

1. Click Start, click Run, and type **\\Computer*p*** in the Open text box (where *p* is your partner's student ID number).
2. Click OK.

   The shares on your partner's computer appear.
3. Double-click the Student*z*Remote share.
4. Double-click Student*z*Remote File.

   What happened?

   _____

5. Leave the file open.

Exercise 4
Viewing the Open Files on Your Computer and Closing All Open Files

In this exercise, you'll use the Computer Management snap-in to view any open files on your local computer and close all open files.

Note Before beginning this exercise, both you and your lab partner must have completed Exercise 3.

▶ **To view the open files on your computer and close all open files**

1. Click Start, click Control Panel, click Performance And Maintenance, click Administrative Tools, and then double-click Computer Management.

2. In the console tree (left pane) of Computer Management, expand System Tools and Shared Folders if necessary, and then click Open Files.

   Are there any open files? If yes, what are the filenames?

   _____

   _____

3. Right-click Open Files, and then click Disconnect All Open Files.

   The Shared Folders message box appears, asking if you are sure you want to close all resources (disconnect all open files).

4. Click Yes.

   What happened?

   _____

Exercise 5
Viewing the Open Sessions on Your Computer

In this exercise, you'll use the Computer Management snap-in to view any sessions open on your local computer.

Note Before beginning this exercise, both you and your lab partner must have completed Exercise 4.

▶ **To view open sessions**

1. In the console tree (left pane) of Computer Management, under Shared Folder, click Sessions.

    Are there any open sessions? If yes, who has an open session, and why?

    _____

    _____

    _____

2. Open WordPad.

3. On the File menu, click Save As, and then save the file as **Student*z*Remote File2** (where *z* is your student ID number).

    Were you able to save the file? Why or why not?

    _____

    _____

    _____

    _____

4. Close Computer Management.
5. Close WordPad.
6. Log off the domain.

Lab 18: Installing and Using the Recovery Console

Objectives

After completing this lab, you will be able to

- Install the Recovery Console from a network share that contains the Microsoft Windows XP Professional installation files
- Use the Recovery Console Help command to view the available commands
- Use the Recovery Console to disable a service
- Use the Computer Management snap-in to configure the Startup Type for a service

Note Completing this lab will reinforce your learning from Chapter 18 of the textbook.

Before You Begin

Before you start this lab, you'll need to know your student ID number, the domain number, and the number assigned to your instructor's computer.

Estimated time to complete the lab: 20 minutes

Exercise 1
Installing the Recovery Console from a Network Share

In this exercise, you'll connect to a network share that contains the Windows XP Professional installation files and then install the Recovery Console on your computer.

▶ **To install the Recovery Console from a network share**

1. Log on to the Corp*y* domain as Student*z* (where *y* is the domain number and *z* is your student ID number).
2. Click Start, and then click Run.

    A Run dialog box appears.

3. In the Open box, type **\\instructor*x*\wxppro** (where *x* is the number assigned to your instructor's computer), and then click OK.

    A window appears, showing the folders in the wxppro share.

4. Double-click the i386 folder.
5. Click Start, and then click Run.
6. In the Run dialog box, type **\\instructor*x*\wxppro\i386\winnt32 /cmdcons** and then click OK.

    A Windows Setup message box appears, indicating that you can install the Windows Recovery Console as a startup option.

7. Click Yes to install the Recovery Console.

    Windows Setup attempts to contact Microsoft (through your Internet connection) and confirm that you have the latest version of Setup. If you receive a message indicating that Windows Setup was unable to contact Microsoft, select Skip This Step And Continue Installing Windows, and then click Next.

    Windows Setup then installs the Windows XP Recovery Console on your hard disk.

    A Microsoft Windows XP Professional Setup message box appears, indicating that the Recovery Console has been successfully installed. It notifies you that you must restart your computer and then select Windows Recovery Console from the Startup menu if you want to use the Recovery Console.

8. Click OK to close the Microsoft Windows XP Professional Setup dialog box.

Exercise 2
Using the Recovery Console

In this exercise, you'll use the Help command to view the available commands in the Recovery Console. Then you'll use the available Listsvc and Disable commands.

▶ **To use the Recovery Console**

1. Click Start, and then click Shut Down.
2. In the What Do You Want The Computer To Do? drop-down list box, select Restart, and then click OK to restart your computer.
3. In the Please Select The Operating System To Start screen, select Microsoft Windows Recovery Console.

   The Recovery Console starts and prompts you to select which Windows installation you would like to log on to. (If you had more than one Windows XP Professional installation on this computer, all of them would be listed.)

4. Type **1** and then press ENTER.
5. Type **password** when prompted for the Administrator password, and then press ENTER.
6. Type **help** and then press ENTER to see the list of available commands.
7. Scroll through the list of commands.
8. Type **listsvc** and press ENTER, and then scroll through the list of available services.
9. Press ESC to stop.
10. Type **disable** and then press ENTER.

    The Disable command lets you disable a Windows system service or driver.

11. Type **disable alerter** and then press ENTER.

    The Recovery Console displays several lines of text describing how the registry entry for the Alerter service has been changed from Service_Demand_Start to Service_Disabled. The Alerter service is now disabled.

12. Type **exit** and then press ENTER to restart your computer.

Exercise 3
Restarting the Alerter Service

In this exercise, you'll use the Computer Management snap-in to reset the Alerter service Startup Type to Automatic.

▶ **To restart the Alerter service**

1. Log on to the local computer as Administrator.
2. Click Start, click All Programs, click Administrative Tools, and then click Computer Management.
3. In the Computer Management window, in the left pane, expand Services And Applications.
4. Under Services And Applications, click Services.
5. Double-click Alerter.
6. In the Alerter Properties dialog box, change the Startup Type option to Automatic, and then click OK.
7. Right-click Alerter, and then click Start.
8. Close the Computer Management window.
9. Log off the local computer.

Lab 19: Converting a Basic Disk

Objectives

After completing this lab, you will be able to

- Convert a basic disk to a dynamic disk

Note Completing this lab will reinforce your learning from Chapter 19 of the textbook.

Estimated time to complete the lab: 15 minutes

Exercise 1
Upgrading a Disk

In this exercise, you'll use Disk Management to upgrade a basic disk to a dynamic disk.

▶ **To upgrade a basic disk**

1. Log on locally to your computer as Fred, who is a member of the Administrators group.
2. Click Start, right-click My Computer, and then click Manage.

    The Computer Management snap-in appears.
3. In the console tree, double-click Storage to expand it (if necessary), and then click Disk Management.

    Notice that the storage type of Disk 0 is Basic.
4. In the lower right pane of the Computer Management window, right-click Disk 0, and then click Convert To Dynamic Disk.

    The Convert To Dynamic Disk dialog box appears.
5. Ensure that Disk 0 is the only disk selected for conversion, and then click OK.

    The Disks To Convert dialog box appears.
6. Click Convert.

    A Disk Management dialog box appears, warning that after this upgrade, you will not be able to boot previous versions of Microsoft Windows from any volume on this disk.
7. Click Yes.

    A Convert Disk dialog box appears, notifying you that file systems on any of the disks to be upgraded will be force dismounted.
8. Click Yes.

    A Confirm message box appears, notifying you that a reboot will take place to complete the upgrade process.
9. Click OK.

Exercise 2
Verifying the Upgrade

In this exercise, you'll use Disk Management to verify that the disk was upgraded from a basic disk to a dynamic disk.

▶ **To confirm the upgrade**

1. Log on locally to your computer as Fred, who is a member of the Administrators group.
2. Click Start, right-click My Computer, and then click Manage.

    The Computer Management snap-in appears.
3. In the console tree, double-click Storage to expand it (if necessary), and then click Disk Management.

    Notice that the storage type of Disk 0 is Dynamic.
4. Close Computer Management, and then log off the computer.